7/0 3

Don't Tell

Don't Tell

The Sexual Abuse of Boys

MICHEL DORAIS

Translated by

ISABEL DENHOLM MEYER

McGill-Queen's University Press
Montreal & Kingston · London · Ithaca

© McGill-Queen's University Press 2002
ISBN 0-7735-2260-3 (cloth)
ISBN 0-7735-2261-1 (paper)

Legal deposit first quarter 2002
Bibliothèque nationale du Québec

Printed in Canada on acid-free paper.

McGill-Queen's University Press acknowledges
the financial support of the Government of Canada
through the Book Publishing Industry Development
Program (BPIDP) for its activities. It also
acknowleges the support of the Canada Council
for the Arts for its publishing program.

This book is available in French under the title *Ça
arrive aussi aux garçons*, published by VLB in 1997.

We gratefully acknowledge the financial support of
Quebec's Société de développement des entreprises
culturelles (SODEC) in the translation of this book.

**National Library of Canada Cataloguing
in Publication Data**

Dorais, Michel, 1954–
   Don't Tell: the sexual abuse of boys
   Translation of: Ça arrive aussi aux garçons.
   Includes bibliographical references and index.
   ISBN 0-7735-2260-3 (bound) –
   ISBN 0-7735-2261-1 (pbk.)
   1. Sexually abused children. 2. Child sexual abuse.
   3. Male sexual abuse victims. 4. Sexually abused
   children – Psychology. 5. Child sexual abuse –
   Psychological aspects. 6. Masculinity (Psychology).
   7. Child sexual abuse – Prevention. I. Meyer, Isabel
   Denholm. II. Title.
   HV6570.D6713 2002   362.76'083'41   C2001-901662-X

Typeset in Palatino 10.5/13
by Caractéra inc., Quebec City

Contents

Acknowledgments

The author thanks Daniel Welzer-Lang for his contribution regarding the "construction of the masculine" and is indebted to Denis Ménard and Normand Ricard of the Centres Jeunesse of Montérégie, who not only encouraged this project but greatly facilitated its realization. The entire team at the original publisher, VLB éditeur, also deserves thanks. The Quebec Council for Social Research made a contribution in awarding the author one of its first post-doctoral research grants to complete this study. Without the great determination and work of Isabel Denholm Meyer, this book wouldn't exist in this english version.

The translator wishes to thank McGill-Queen's editor Aurèle Parisien for his support for this community service project. The McGill-Queen's copy editor was invaluable in refining the translation into English of some of the Quebecois language. British poet Pamela Gillilan collaborated over a period of ten days in the joyous struggle to tease out and convey finer meanings here and there.

Author's Preface

As a researcher and an author, I rarely seem to have chosen the subjects about which I write. Rather, the subjects present themselves to me and force me to pay attention to them.

When I began my research into the sexual abuse of boys, I hardly suspected how vast or complex the subject would be. Neither did I foresee the quandaries, dilemmas, and questions that would come to me as I worked. Having been involved for several years with child survivors of sexual abuse, I thought I understood them. I was wrong. In the course of this study I discovered an unexplored universe, where the reality of sufferings and silences calls into question the whole significance of what it is to be a man. I also learned that many, many boys have been sexually molested.

Knowing the research in which I was engaged, men close to me and even acquaintances confided in me, revealing that fifteen, thirty, sixty years ago, they too had "gone through that." They were opening up about it for the first time. The sexual aggression they had undergone during their childhood or adolescence still remains the deepest of all their wounds and their most guarded secret.

The situations described in this book are often disturbing and the language is sometimes crude. However, I have refused to censor what I heard. Since it is impossible to remain neutral, faced with such a subject, I have had no hesitation in addressing the reader directly myself. In so doing, I have followed the example of those who have made it possible for me to write this book. May my writing be true to them.

The distress of boy victims of sexual abuse appeals to us to make creative responses to their needs. Researchers, social workers, and child protection agencies have much work to do if they wish to improve the effectiveness of their preventive and healing efforts.

Several respondents have expressed the hope that their testimony will help other victims to better understand themselves and will sensitize the public to the realities tied to the sexual abuse of boys. Let us hope their wish is not in vain.

This book consists of two parallel texts. The narratives quote twelve of the young men I interviewed, giving lengthy extracts from their life stories as they told them to me in detail, and those stories link the chapters of the book. It seemed unthinkable to recount the male experience of sexual abuse without including the words of those primarily concerned. The narratives chosen meet four criteria: each one presents situations that relate to the themes dealt with in the adjacent chapters; each illustrates different types of sexual abuse; together they convey the diversity of the abuse experience and the reactions of the boys to such abuse. I have been careful to present the testimonies so that they reflect different times in the lives of the ex-victims, i.e., adolescence, early adulthood, maturity. There seems to be a different and yet complementary, resonance to the telling of the story, depending on how recently or how long ago it happened.

All the cases quoted in this text are factual. Secondary information was, however, modified to protect the anonymity of the respondents. For this reason, those whom I interviewed were requested to provide a fictitious first name. Any exact similarity to persons living or dead is therefore purely by chance.

Readers looking for more detailed profiles of the boys who took part in this research, or who need a more detailed description of the methodology employed in gathering and analyzing their testimonies, should refer to Appendix 1 and Appendix 2.

Translator's Preface

The title of Michel Dorais' book – *Ça arrive aussi aux garçons: l'abus sexuel au masculin* – jumped out at me from the shelf as I was leaving the local pharmacy one day in 1997. Sexual abuse in childhood had played an important part in my son's deciding to end his life in 1991. I recognised Paul on many pages of chapter 7. He had struggled along a lonely road for many years, unable to let anyone know that, from the age of eleven, he was being sexually abused by a man living in the neighbourhood (but a stranger to the family) to whom he delivered the morning newspaper.

Paul was twenty-five by the time he was enabled to disclose what had happened to him by a caring psychosynthesis therapist to whom we both had turned for help in understanding the difficulties in our relationship. Paul had been unaware that other boys go through similar trauma: the confusions, the anger, the pain, and the addictions, although he had empathized with women who had been abused in childhood. In psychosynthesis therapy for a year, Paul made positive strides toward understanding his situation. Gradually, however, it became clear that medication was indicated. Psychiatric service's were sought but at twenty-nine, on his third attempt, Paul succeeded in taking his life.

Michel Dorais has given us an account of what thirty adolescent and grown-up boy victims of sexual abuse and its aftermath have told him about their life experiences. My goal and sincere desire in translating this French language text for the English speaking community is firstly to bring about a greater awareness of the widespread incidence of the sexual abuse of young boys and a fuller understanding of the often devastating results. My intention is also to sensitize professionals, families, and others to the need of male survivors "to be held in dignity and heard with the heart" (Olga Denisko, Paul's psychosynthesis therapist). In other words, I hope, by making Michel Dorais's book available to a larger audience, to make a difference in the way society treats boys and grown-up boys who have undergone such experiences.

Research over the past fifteen years has demonstrated that the sexual abuse of boys goes on far more frequently than we have previously realized. The crimes being gradually uncovered in educational, religious, and sports institutions are only a sampling of what has been going on for years, regularly and frequently, in society as a whole. Sexual abuse is being perpetrated on boys as well as girls in homes, families, and neighbourhoods, by close adult relatives and other people in whom a child should be able to fully place his trust.

Women have called their sexual abuse in childhood "soul murder," and many women and girls have learned to speak up about such abuse and to help each other. Most boys, on the other hand, have learned that "to be a man" in our culture means that one must always be strong, never show feelings, allow vulnerability, admit defeat or shame. All those boys and men who have not yet spoken up about their abuse in childhood must be enabled to break their silence too. If they have tried to speak about it and have not been believed, then their need is even greater. They need to understand their experiences in order to move on with their lives. Inability to share the dreadful secret ensures their entrapment and continued abuse. Silence compounds the aftermath, not only for the victim but for his loved ones and sometimes for the broader society as well.

Reading this book is not easy, and may re-open painful wounds. If it does, I strongly encourage you to seek professional help. One of the important reasons behind my undertaking this translation was that Dorais's work sheds some caring light on the difficulties faced by young male victims who often, for too many years, as was the case with my son Paul, regard themselves as completely isolated in their dilemma and are afraid to seek out help.

THIS BOOK IS NOT ONLY FOR MALE VICTIMS AND PROFESSION-ALS. It should be read by victims' family members, friends, teachers, counsellors. It is for police, health workers, for anyone in whom a victim or former victim might confide. The incidence of this abuse is such that most of us probably know a young man, or perhaps even a much older individual, who has undergone this trauma and has not yet been able to disclose it. In short, everyone needs to know what is in this book.

There are important things for victims, those close to victims, professionals, and potential abusers to take from this book. Victims should realize that they have the right to demand help and support no matter how long ago the abuse took place. The accounts in this book make clear that whatever the abuser may have told you, the abuse was not your fault. The friends of victims or anyone who is confided in by a victim should be more able to listen caringly, to support him, and encourage and aid him in seeking professional help.

Hopefully this book will give professionals more awareness of the particular dynamics surrounding the sexual abuse of boys and encourage their active input: services in this area need to be improved, more research needs to be undertaken and published, public workshops need to be available to both colleagues and the public. It is also my hope that anyone who has been, is, or is concerned about becoming, an abuser of boys may be helped by this book to understand the effects and sources of their actual or potential acts. You also need to seek help and will need support in doing so.

If help for men sexually abused in childhood is not included in local phone books, services for children or for women can be contacted for a referral. Self-support groups for older male victims are beginning to appear and occasionally a group may be open to both men and women. If no explicit services can be found for male sexual abuse in childhood, don't give up. Ask a family doctor to provide a referral for social services or to suggest what options are available.

Don't Tell

CHAPTER ONE

Don't Tell Anyone

Such is the warning, or rather the threat, made by a man or an adolescent to the boy he has just sexually abused. Curiously, when the child unveils this secret for the first time, he often uses the same words: "Don't tell anyone." The child seems to believe it is in his best interest to keep the information a close secret. He is all too aware of the taboos pertaining to the abuse of boys by older males: the taboo around the vulnerability of males, the taboo against homosexuality, and the taboo against the involvement of minors in sexual behaviour. The boy will have kept to himself for a long, long time his bewilderment over the "why" of the abuse and his wondering about how to get out of it. Years later, when the child is grown up and dares to take the risk of confiding in someone, he will still not be without fear.

When I was a practising social worker (from the late 1970s to the end of the 1980s) I worked with many boys who were victims of sexual abuse. Despite my attempts to understand the dynamics at work in those cases, many questions persisted. How are male victims of sexual abuse affected by it? How much does the trauma affect their learning and their emotional development? What are the consequences of such sexual abuse on their future behaviour, their sexual orientation, and their sexual identity? Why do some of them reproduce with younger children the abuse they themselves have suffered? From the limited research and studies available at the time, I found few answers to my questions. It was then that I began to formulate early ideas for the present research – well before the finalized project was decided and well before I became a professional researcher. What compelled me to actually carry out this research is more personal. Being involved in the daily lives of relatives who were formerly victims of sexual abuse cannot help but raise serious questions, nourish continuing reflection, and encourage intense discussion. This work is the outcome.

The reality to be faced on the following pages is not new, and yet little has been written about the sexual abuse of boys. The sexual abuse of males in childhood remains a poorly understood phenomenon and the extent to which it occurs seems to be underestimated. To date, very few researchers have taken an interest in this reality, even although it is recognized that a large proportion of boys showing behavioural problems (for example, delinquency, drug abuse) have been victims of sexual abuse during their childhood or adolescence. It is only after weeks, months, even years of therapy that such victims may be able to share their secret and the uneasy feelings that accompany it. Where the secret has not been shared, and where, consequently, the victims have received no understanding, reassurance or support, some of them may, in turn, victimize others, reproducing with younger children the sexual abuse they themselves experienced. It is as if their silence and our ignorance combine to maintain a repetitive cycle of sexual abuse.

Although we are beginning to perceive the physical, sexual and relationship effects of sexual abuse on boys, a comprehensive and complex awareness of the phenomenon is still embryonic. Specialists observe that fear, anxiety, negative self-image and low self-esteem, abuse of alcohol or drugs, violence directed against the self or others, and a tendency toward depression and suicide as well as toward a problematic sexuality are prevalent in the life histories of the victims, but we do not know how these after-effects develop and link together. We also underestimate the repercussions of sexual abuse on the essential dimension of individual stability or even on the building of the person's self-identity. As I see it, identity loss or identity confusion seem to underlie the main problems experienced by men who were sexually abused as children.

In her study on the make-up of the masculine identity, Elizabeth Badinter[1] has shown that to fit the masculine model of virility, a boy must convince himself and others that he is no longer a child (neither dependent nor vulnerable), that he is not a woman (neither passive nor effeminate), and that he is not homosexual (and thus feels no attraction towards other men). Now here lies a predicament for the young male victim of sexual aggression. He has been, and may still feel, vulnerable; he has been taken "like a woman" (at least according to certain cultural stereotypes); and he has also been involved in a homosexual type of relationship.

Starting from these premises, and allowing those most affected to speak, I wanted to learn how the experience of sexual abuse influences the formation of masculine identity. In other words, I wanted to know what effect sexual abuse has on the way abused boys see themselves and how they see sexuality. What self-searching and distress must these boys face up to during and after the abuse they have suffered? In what way do they try to preserve their feelings of virility? My aim was to suggest approaches to intervention methods for prevention of abuse and its consequences in light of the responses obtained.

My intent was to bring out the defining characteristics in the lives of thirty or so boys who had been sexually molested by other males, whether adolescents or adults. It was a question not only of examining the psychological, behavioural, and relational consequences to the young men of having been sexually abused but also of showing the evolution of such consequences. I wanted in particular to ascertain how their experience of sexual abuse had affected their self-perception, how it affected their perception of others, and how such perceptions influenced their behaviours. I was equally preoccupied by the question whether boys who have been violated are inclined to replicate the abuse they have experienced, and if so, why. In short, I wanted to understand what it is these men feel and how they deal with their trauma.

My goal, and I cannot emphasize it enough, was not to describe, as others have done before, all the possible consequences arising from sexual abuse between males. My objective was rather to make connections between the different after-effects of abuse and, as far as possible, find a logic in it. For example, are certain ways of life adopted or certain typical adaptations made by boys who have been victims of sexual aggression? Such questions forced me to go beyond a simple description of the phenomena in order to interpret them and, indeed, to attempt to explain them.

Thirty young men who had been victims of sexual abuse in childhood or adolescence were interviewed in strict confidence. They all fitted the following criterion: they had, as they saw it, been sexually abused during childhood or the very beginning of adolescence by an older adolescent male or adult male. The average age of the respondents at the time of interview was 24.5 years. Half were between sixteen and twenty-five, the other half between twenty-five and forty-four. Their average age at time of first abuse was eight years and four months. They were all fourteen or less at the time of this first abuse; some were only four or five years old. About two-thirds of the respondents were victims of incestuous abuse, either by a natural father or substitute father (twelve cases); an older brother (five cases); an uncle (three cases); a grandfather (one case); or by a cousin (one case). More than one-third were violated by people who, while not related to them, were generally known to the boy or to his family. In nine of these cases adults were involved and in the other four cases adolescents older than the victim were involved.[2]

It will have been noted that I have limited my research to abuse between males, assuming, rightly or wrongly, that such cases possess a particular dynamic that brings especially into question the sexual identity and the sexual orientation of the victims.[3] Abuse of boys by older males is reported more frequently than abuse by females, which suggests either that it is indeed more common, or that possibly sexual abuse of boys by females is more easily tolerated in general. Some respondents have stated that such a situation would have seemed more "normal" to them. Experts in this subject are divided in their opinions, although abuses committed by females are of increasing interest to researchers, who are inclined to agree that such cases are underreported.[4]

It is important to define at the outset the terms used in this text. Firstly, what is sexual abuse? For the purposes of this study I define sexual abuse of children as removal of clothing, sexual touching, or sexual relations between people who are different in age and power, both physically and psychologically. These activities are not solicited by the younger children or adolescents, who are manipulated by abuse of trust, blackmail, coercion, threat, or violence. Other definitions exist. According to Daniel Welzer-Lang,[5] sexual abuse consists of a situation of dominance in which the person in the dominant position imposes sexual activities on the other. For authors Watkins and Bentovim,[6] it consists of implicating dependent and immature children or adolescents in sexual activities they do not truly understand, for which they are unable to give well-informed consent, and which, at least in the case of incest, violate taboos and accepted family roles.

The definition I propose has the advantage of not putting stress on violence alone and of taking into account a control facilitated by the difference in age and power between the victim and the aggressor. There is certainly a difference between abuse constituting sadistic or violent aggression on the one hand and abuse that, on the face of it, is more subtle, where the aggressor, by means of various subterfuges, gradually leads the child to participate in a sexual act. But in either case the child is disadvantaged by the ability of the older to impose his desire and the difficulty of the child to oppose it. Sexual abuse of whatever description always presents the same dynamic: that a child, directly or indirectly, is obliged to participate in sexual acts. In short, sexual abuse always implies a sexual relationship imposed by an adult or an adolescent on a child or a younger adolescent, against the latter's will, or by obtaining his participation by ruse, lies, force, or fear (whatever the degree of physical, moral, or psychological constraint employed).

Although relatively clear, this definition nevertheless requires clarification. Sometimes, the boys will consider themselves to be participating voluntarily in the sexual activities introduced by an older male. Does this then allow us to speak of "participating victims," or indeed to stop considering such situations as abusive? Not necessarily. Such situations only demonstrate that it is difficult to separate people into victims who are one hundred percent passive and aggressors who are one hundred percent active. As we shall see, diverse gratifications are possible one way or another even in a context of abuse. Some boys were particularly vulnerable because they were interested in exploring a situation that presented itself to them, whether it was getting closer to someone they were fond of, satisfying their sexual curiosity, or simply not displeasing their aggressor. What characterizes the abuse in such cases is that the experience goes far beyond what the child anticipated, and, more importantly, beyond what he was ready to agree to or go through.

Where abuse between boys of different ages is concerned – the elder taking advantage of the younger – precise categorization is just as difficult. A relationship of strength or power is often less evident in such cases than when the abuser is an adult. At times, the curiosity or participation of the victim is obvious. Some boys assert that they did not consider they had been abused until much later. It can be difficult to distinguish between sexual exploration between peers and an abusive situation: it is a question of the balance or imbalance of power between the partners, a question of perception. Ultimately, only the young people themselves can discern the precise nature of their coming together. Sometimes, the panic of the parents or educators seems to attach more to the homosexual nature of the reported activity than to any other aspect. It must be remembered that games of a homosexual nature played by boys do not automatically imply sexual aggression. Sexual abuse has nothing to do with the sexual identity or the sexual orientation, affirmed or presumed, of the protagonists. Rather, it has to do with the context surrounding their relationship. Let us agree, being sexual is not in itself damaging.

For purposes of this study, I have assumed that an abuse has occurred between peers when the younger has been coerced into complying or continuing to participate against his will in the sexual activities demanded of him. Sometimes, as in the case of two respondents who were subjugated by the desires of an older brother, it is only years later, when time has provided perspective and critical faculties are more highly developed, that what had been considered to be an exchange of friendly services comes to be recognized as being abusive.

As to whether egalitarian sexual relations can exist between adults and minors, it is not for me to pronounce, although some authors claim that intergenerational sexuality may be without after-effects.[7] This study does not deal with intergenerational sexuality in a general way.

Most Western legislators have fixed the age of sexual consent at fourteen years and over because it seems very difficult to claim that anyone below this age can give fully enlightened consent. The physical and psychological imbalance that exists between an adult and a child of less than fourteen years is almost enough to justify this measure. Add to this the more obvious imbalance between the power and resources of an adult compared to those of a child and it is clear that intimate relations between the two can scarcely be deemed egalitarian. Nevertheless, there are testimonies that affirm the contrary. A recent Dutch film, based on an auto-biographical novel, *For a Lost Soldier*, tells of such a liaison. Reality or fiction? Readers will have their own opinion.

According to some, the growing emphasis on the protection of children and repeated warnings about sexual aggression may in themselves perturb young people almost as much, at times, as the evil they warn against.[8] I agree that we must avoid frightening or worrying children with our adult fears. There is certainly a wide divergence between a healthy prevention or intervention based on the needs of the child, and a moral panic that sees sexual abuse in the most harmless conduct. To foster or encourage such panic is in no way the intention of this work. Reality is already disquieting enough.

PASCAL'S STORY

Pascal was sexually abused by a friend of the family when he was seven or eight years old.

I'm seventeen. I look like an ordinary guy, quite proper, even if I'm not always. I'm like a chameleon. Sometimes I take on another personality because I'm afraid of what people will think of me if I'm really myself.

I was pushed around from one place to another when I was little. My grandmother looked after me when I was born. After I was two, I lived with different relatives for about five years, but I never stayed in one place more than about a year. Then I was in foster homes. That's when I found out my real mother wasn't who I thought she was. They'd always told me my aunt was my real mother. In other words, I thought my mother's sister was my mother. I didn't know who my father was, either. I still don't know. I always thought it was my uncle. But no. I realized my mother and the whole family were lying to me. It's hard to accept that. It really shocked me to realize how much they all lied to me.

I began getting into trouble, became a delinquent. I saw a social worker after that. I really hated adults.

When I was about seven or eight years old and in a foster home, a friend of my mother started coming to see me to take me out or to play hockey. He was the only one who showed any interest in me at that time. He was about thirty years old, a bit like a father for me. I got quite attached to him; I saw him as someone who took care of me. He was like a friend I always had a good time with. Each visit was like a gift in a way.

At the beginning, we only had body contact when he was teasing me or tickling me. That's okay. We were simply playing together. It was later, when he tried to touch me lower down, that everything changed.

In my memory, the abuse was not necessarily violent. Just touching. I went along with it so as not to disappoint him. Afterwards, I took off, running. I realized what had happened was not right. It happened behind the trees in a huge park where we had gone to play together. He had taken me in his arms and was tickling me. Then his hands went down my

body. I was thinking, what on earth is he doing? Surely he's
going to stop. He doesn't know what he's doing. I was asking
myself serious questions. That first time, I didn't even ask
myself if he was doing it for his own pleasure, or if he had
homosexual tendencies or whatever. I told myself he wasn't in
his right mind, that he didn't usually behave that way, that perhaps he'd had something to drink or had taken drugs. It was
only the second time, the next day I think, that I told myself he
could be doing it intentionally, that he could enjoy doing that.
I could see he didn't want to hurt me. Something else, it never
occurred to me to cry out, even though we were outdoors.
I didn't want him to get caught. I let him get on with it, knowing he would let me take off after he had done what he wanted.

But I didn't like it. On later occasions he saw that I was
resisting. He distanced himself from me. He didn't speak to me
as he had done before, he didn't take me out anymore. On the
one hand, that hurt me, but on the other hand I was pleased;
I didn't want him to start up again. From one day to the next it
was if he had abandoned me. Perhaps he felt the same about
me, I don't know, but I didn't want to see him again, even if
I did miss him. Before, he was a role model for me. Since then
I've replaced him with others.

I tell myself I should denounce him, but I find all sorts of reasons not to. I can't do it. I tell myself maybe he did it because
he just wanted to try it out; he only did it with me because the
opportunity was there, because he saw me often, because we
played games together, because we were quite close. But when
all is said and done, he did nothing but hurt me. I never found
the answer to why he had done it. I should stop asking myself
the question. I've been obsessing over it for too long.

Even if he didn't come to take me out again, I saw him all
the same when I went to my mother's place at the weekend.
I loved him, I still do in spite of everything, I think. I don't see
him anymore, but I hear about him indirectly. I don't know if
he does the same thing with others. I have the impression it
was only with me he made this mistake. In any case, I loved
him too much to denounce him. He probably knows this. I was
afraid he would be rejected by the whole family, that no one
would speak to him and that he would go to prison. That's
why I didn't speak up.

At school, when they were warning us about strangers, about paedophiles, I said I wanted to go to the bathroom and left the classroom: I didn't want to hear about that. It's not true anyway: it wasn't a stranger who abused me, it was someone I knew. He was my friend, someone I felt good with. Most of the guys I know who have been abused were abused in their family, by their father or their uncle. I found out that my grandfather was also an abuser. He did it with his daughters. I found out recently. Perhaps it's him who's my father.

I had a huge reaction to being abandoned by adults. First it was my own family and them him. I felt bad all the time. I didn't know what to think of the world. I didn't go to school any more, even if I was only eight or nine years old. I stole. I wanted to have some effect on people, make them have a reaction like I was made to react. In spite of it all, there was one uncle I could be close to. In the evenings I ran away to be with him. I wanted to live with him, but when we tried it didn't work out. Everyone was against it. I was heartbroken. I started to do really bad things. I stole car radios, I stole from stores. I was stealing from cars and I was only twelve! I was working for a group of car thieves. They became like my family. When I ran away from home, I could sleep over with them. It was useful.

When I was around fifteen, I was in a foster family where there was a little girl six years old. I did with her the same thing that had happened to me: I caressed her and I masturbated myself. It was in the evening, I had done drugs, it was a spur of the moment thing. I had just had quite a squabble with my girlfriend. Perhaps I wanted to take it out on someone else, I don't know. She was asleep the first time. The next morning, I started again. This time she woke up and she saw what I was doing. I took off.

When the foster mother found out about it, after the little girl had spoken up, I tried to explain myself. I was accused of sexual abuse and was sent to a group home after that, even if it never went to court, for lack of evidence I think. I was willing to get help. I realize that what happened was a result of the sexual abuse I had gone through. It's as though I wanted to get some revenge on someone younger. The only difference is that I had chosen a girl because it's girls who attract me. It was totally unpremeditated.

I have never had violent fantasies. I'm more the romantic type. I try not to think of the abuse I committed because I might have a tendency to do it again if the occasion presented itself, but I have forbidden myself to do that. I have taken tests which say I'm oriented towards girls of the same age or younger than myself. Homosexuality is not my bag. If I were homosexual I would accept it, but I go for women.

I must admit I've had fantasies about younger boys also. At a certain point I had a dream: I was abusing a young fellow the way I was abused. That's really not my thing. I reacted badly. It was as though I'd been hit on the head with a sledgehammer. I thought of killing myself. I cut my veins. But I stopped in time. This went on for about eight or nine months. I said to myself: If I'm capable of doing it in a dream I could do it awake. But I don't want to be involved with young boys. I'm in therapy for that. I try not to think of the past. It's like putting on a suit of armour. I've had other similar dreams recently, with girls in the dreams too. I wake up and I feel excited. But now, instead of panicking, I try to make the connections. I ask myself what happened the day before to make me think of that. I keep a journal to help me understand, to make the connections between it all.

Right now I don't have a girlfriend. When I had one, we had sexual relations and both of us were satisfied. Finally, I think I'm normal. When I go out with a girl, I take my time: I wait three or four months before doing anything sexual. Once we get into it, I have to make her happy, satisfy her. It's very important to me. What doesn't help is that I'm still mistrustful of others. At night, my door has to be locked, my window properly closed. I lived with a girl once for three weeks. Even if she was my girlfriend, I couldn't sleep beside her. I went to sleep all alone in the living-room. I don't trust anyone. With guys, it's even worse. Even in my family, since we became closer, I still can't manage to sleep there. I tell myself perhaps they are abusers too. It's crazy but that's the way it is. Before, even a police siren didn't wake me; today, a breath of air is enough to startle me when I am sleeping.

It's in the morning, when I get up, that's the worst time. No one must see me, no one must touch me. At a certain point an educator came to shake me and wake me up because I was late.

Even if he only touched my arm it immediately made me think
of my abuser. I'm only just beginning to trust adults. It's three
years I've been in the group home and it's only in the last three
months that I can talk about myself, about what happened to
me. I had a big drug problem: mescaline, acid, coke. I wanted
to die. I'm pretty suicidal deep down. I still get thoughts like
that. When I get too agitated, I lose control, I can't calm myself
down any more.

I'm afraid of men, especially drunk men. I ask myself
whether they're abusers. You never know what could happen.
Often, men on the street who are more or less drunk will offer
money to young people, saying "Come on, I'll suck you off, I'll
give you five bucks." It happened to me. I think most kids have
experienced that. Me, I clear off when it happens. I find them
idiotic to say that. Perhaps it's the drink, I don't know. If they
really want to do that, at least they should ask properly. They
should wait until they are sobered up the next day and they
should do it with guys who are into that kind of thing. As for
me, I want some respect. Let them do what they want, but
me … Some of them make me aggressive, some less so, maybe
because of their appearance: I tell myself they've got problems.
Some of them are really pathetic.

Today I feel I'm trying to bury the past. I tell myself that it
happened because I was too little. I took karate, lots of sports.
I've become quite hefty. I would take off if he tried it again.
Perhaps I would hit him too. But I wouldn't denounce him. No.
On that I haven't changed my mind, because he wasn't such
a bad guy. If I saw him again today, I would just take him to
have a beer and I would ask him some questions. I would ask
him what on earth got into his head when he did that to me.
Is it because it happened to him when he was little?

Many guys here, in the group home, have gone through
being abused. We help each other, we speak about it sometimes between ourselves. I don't feel alone any more. Most of
them reacted pretty much as I did. It's strange, but most of my
friends have been abused and I've learned about it after we've
become friends. It's as though we sensed we had something
in common.

At the time it happened to me, I didn't understand what it
was all about. Even today, if someone talks to me about abuse,

it's all gobbledegook to me. I pretend to understand, but when others tell me their stories, it's as though I avoid looking back, avoid thinking too much about it. With my girlfriends, I never speak about the abuse. I tell myself that if they find out, okay, but I prefer not to talk about it.

I'm reading a book about how to say no to sexual harassment. Today for the first time I can understand what the social worker is telling me. There are some people, you could say they do it on purpose so you won't understand them when they speak about abuse.

I like it when people accept me as I am. It helps me to talk. Boys who've been sexually abused should be helped to talk about it as soon as it happens to them, not have to wait ten years before they can open up. If not, it grows bigger, like a snowball inside you.

When I'm older, I picture myself as a loner. I would like to be a truck driver, a night bird, to be free, travelling the highway. Otherwise, I will have a family, maybe. That's important for someone like me who never had one. It's as if I have something to prove to my mother …

CHAPTER TWO

It Never Happens to Boys?

For a long time, it was thought that sexual abuse of boys was still a marginal phenomenon. This is not so. Within the past few years North American researchers have found that one out of six boys is a victim of sexual abuse. In a Canadian national survey carried out for the Badgley Commission in the early 1980s,[1] it was found that, in a sample of 1,002 Canadian males, 30.6 percent reported having undergone unwanted sexual acts ranging from exhibition-ism to sexual touching to threats of violence and rape. Looking more closely at these findings, about sixteen percent of male respondents – that is, one-sixth – reported that they had been victims of sexual touching or aggression by older boys or men before they reached the age of eighteen. These figures match the findings of other North American studies completed at the same time or later.[2] A national survey carried out in the United States in 1990 reported precisely the same results – i.e., sixteen percent of the respondents had already been victims of sexual abuse.[3]

Among certain more vulnerable subgroups of the male popu-lation, the proportion of sexual abuse victims is even higher. A survey for the Badgley Commission of 229 young male prostitutes showed that for one in three of the boys, their first sexual activity took place during an act of sexual aggression. Another more recent study conducted by Queen's University researchers shows that, among the young Canadians interviewed, prostitutes and drug addicts were the most likely to have experienced early sexual relations in a context of abuse.[4] Several American and British studies confirm this correlation in a conclusive manner.[5] Boys of homosexual or bisexual orientation were also more likely to have been subjected to sexual aggression. According to an enquiry carried out among its readers by the gay magazine *The Advocate*, twenty-one percent of respondents did in fact consider they had been victims of sexual abuse before the age of sixteen.[6] I shall come back to this topic.

Two tendencies show up in the existing statistics on sexual abuse among boys. Firstly, the more recent the research, the higher the incidence of abuse: with growing social awareness of the phenomenon, it seems that more men are willing to disclose their secret. And again, the broader the definition of sexual abuse, the higher the number of people confirming that they have been victims of such abuse. I should add that the boy-girl ratio for abuse is generally held to be about 1:2. Sexual abuse of boys accounts for somewhat less than one-third of all reported cases.[7] But this figure does not take into account the fact that boys are more reluctant than girls to disclose the fact that they have been abused. There are several reasons for this. Because boys are more inclined to conceal their hurts, the physical and emotional trauma of abuse is less visible in boys. They are also aware of the sexist prejudice whereby adults are more reluctant to acknowledge that a boy can be sexually molested. Moreover, as noted earlier, the masculine conception of virility is incompatible with the factual experience of having been a victim of sexual abuse, or of needing help following such a trauma: the assumption is that a "real man" would not allow himself to be dependent, vulnerable, weak, or passive; that a "real" man knows how to avoid problems or would at least be able to get himself out of a difficult situation.

There are other reasons. Young fellows, more so than girls, are encouraged to explore their bodies, or the bodies of others, which could open the way to abuse (whether as victim or abuser). Thus, young boys might tend to consider sexual touching or even sexual abuse as part of sexual initiation. Boys who have been abused might also harbour guilt for having derived some sexual pleasure from their ordeal, for having had an erection or ejaculating or receiving some reward (attention, gifts, money, or drugs) – gestures that might make it seem that they were willing victims. It might be the victim himself who perceives his experience in this way, but the perception could also be instilled by family, or possibly by a social worker or police officer.

Like most people, young men regard homosexuality as a taboo subject and therefore remain silent about any abuse of a homosexual nature. Their silence, however, stems more from the fear that they will be blamed for having accepted, sought out, or provoked contact in the first place, or accused of having enjoyed it. If a child, whatever his age, is suspected of having a homosexual orientation, he may even be accused of having "seduced" the adult. The incident will then be seen as a homosexual initiation. The myth of abuse as initiation is persistent because a certain number of abused boys will indeed develop homosexual or bisexual orientations.

A boy who has been abused will frequently feel ambivalent towards the aggressor, with whom, in most cases, he is already acquainted and to whom he feels some connection; hence a reticence to denounce the aggressor's behaviour. The sexual aggressor is frequently related to the young person and may indeed be someone he looks up to. Even when this is not the case, sexual abuse may be tolerated in silence because it is seen as an occasion to be close to a father or brother who is otherwise distant, indifferent, or even violent.

Boys who have been abused find themselves doubly constrained: if they reveal that they have been abused when they have previously shown no sign of it, they may be thought to be lying. Conversely, if signs of traumatization have already surfaced, it may be thought that they are seeking through such a revelation to blame someone else for their own bad behaviour. They are not likely to be taken any more seriously.

Almost all the respondents who took part in this study reported that they had been reluctant to disclose the abuse they had suffered. It took weeks, months, years, in some cases decades before they could overcome their fear and bring an end to their silence. Of course, threats made by the aggressor to discourage the child from speaking out had their effects. For example, Jean-Philippe's uncle threatened to get involved sexually with his sister if he did not comply; Francis's father said he would leave his wife if his son did not give him what his wife refused him; Bruno's stepfather said he would do nothing for Bruno if he didn't obey him. It should be emphasized, however, that in the long run it is not so much the imminent threat that operates but its interiorization: even when the aggressor is no longer present and no longer threatening, the anxiety implanted in the consciousness of his victim continues to do its work.

The reaction of the young person's family to his disclosure of the abuse preoccupies him as much, if not more, than the threats that are designed to keep him quiet: will they believe me or will they believe the denials of the other? Will they really do something to help me or will they punish me for having talked about it? Unfortunately, this last fear is often borne out. A large number of the young men I questioned were not believed, while several were indeed punished for having offered up such "insanities" concerning a brother, father, uncle, grandfather, or other close family member. Even among the youngest, there are those whose families have made them feel so guilty, if not rejected, after their disclosure of abuse that their family ties have been all but severed. One adolescent was accused of dirtying the memory of his grandfather, who had recently died. This boy was now suicidal.

Many respondents affirmed that no steps were taken to ensure that the disclosed abuse would stop. Mothers declared they would "speak with" their incestuous husbands, but nothing changed. Older brothers, taken into confidence by their younger siblings, promised they would warn a certain uncle not to start up again but didn't keep their word. And how many social workers, police officers, Crown prosecutors, or judges have rejected or thrown out such accusations, leaving a young person all alone in his predicament "for lack of evidence"?

Incest cases are still the most problematic. When the mother has chosen to believe her husband, the boy frequently finds himself isolated from his family, punished for having revealed what was going on, placed in a group home under the pretext of having "behavioural problems." This was confirmed, with bitterness, by one of the boys, Jimmy, aged sixteen, a victim of sexual abuse since he was seven years old: "It's me that's being punished for having accused my father. It's me that's locked up, that can't see my family any more, who's doing time like a prisoner. My mum won't talk to me because she doesn't want me to speak out against my father. My father, who makes out that what he did wasn't so bad, doesn't want to see me either."

The anticipated disbelief, denial, and rejection that have pushed these boys into silence for so long often become too real once the abuse is disclosed. It is not surprising that, after such experiences, these young boys sometimes lock themselves up in their silence and pretend that nothing has happened to them. Let's listen to Bruno, who was sexually abused from the age of six to fourteen: "After I had spoken about it to my mother, nothing happened. I think she was afraid it would break up her marriage. Perhaps, too, she didn't know what to do. Afterwards, I just had to put up with it."

Jean-Philippe, abused since he was nine years old, said: "My older brother had promised he would confront my uncle, but he didn't seem to do anything. I saw that it was useless to speak up about it. People reacted as if it was normal." Maxim, twenty-two years old, abused from eight to twelve years of age, said: "The lady at the group home knew what her husband was doing. I had told her more than once. She always said that it had been dealt with and it would never happen again. That was untrue."

In many cases brought to my attention during the course of this research, the courts, when it went that far, demanded such a preponderance of evidence that the word of the boy had insufficient weight when set against that of the aggressor. Imagine the confusion of a child or adolescent who, having braved fears, threats, and constraints, dares to reveal that he is molested only, in the end, to be labelled a liar. Many young respondents have found themselves disappointed, bitter, and indignant upon such flagrant denial of justice, particularly when it is added to the stress of having to testify repeatedly before police, lawyers, and the courts. Eric, a victim from the age of six, recounted: "At court, the judge refused to continue the hearing because it seemed I was contradicting myself all the time about the dates. How can you remember all of it, and perfectly, especially when you are abused from the age of five or six and you're not even fourteen yet! During long periods of my life I was forced to forget in order to survive. And I got the blame for it!"

Serge, molested at seven years of age, said "I was questioned for hours by police who were saying that it was absolutely necessary to tell everything, all the details. That's what I did, but I've never heard any more about it. I kept on meeting the fellow in the village. I tried to avoid him, but it was not always possible, not until he moved." Maxim, abused from the age of eight, concludes: "In court, as I was remembering it all, I was crying too much to have my wits about me. That was fine by the accused, who didn't get much of a sentence. I figured that, at the most, he did a few minutes of prison for each time he abused me. You call that justice?"

It is not rare to encounter adolescents or men who, having been rebuffed while they were trying to disclose their secret, kept silent afterwards for many, many years. Some respondents assured me they hadn't confided in anyone for ten, fifteen, or even twenty years. The feeling of deliverance they got from doing so had often influenced their decision to participate in this research by sharing their testimony. Although I always felt reticent about asking these men to recall some very painful memories, almost all of them stressed how liberating our conversation had been: at last they had felt free to tell it all, without censure or fear. At last someone had listened to them and believed them. At last someone had been interested in their story, recognized that "the unspeakable" existed and confirmed that they were not alone in what had happened to them, that they were not monsters.

It is remarkable to what extent the sexual abuse of boys – particularly if committed by someone close to them in the family – continues to be denied. The situation has not, it seems, changed very much since Freud abandoned his theory of seduction, which scandalized his peers by recognizing the reality of such aggressions.[8] If society's reluctance to admit the existence of sexual abuse is not new, I would have hoped that there would be less reluctance today. Yet the situation evoked by the youngest respondents hardly differs from that described by the eldest. The politics of silence, perfect accomplice of those who abuse children, persists right up to this day.

At the beginning of my research, I asked respondents essentially the same questions, no matter what the nature of the abuse they were describing. I soon realized that different types of abuse evoke relatively specific reactions and bring about certain specific after-effects. The determining factor seemed to be the type of relationship existing between the aggressor and his victim. Intrafamilial, extrafamilial, intergenerational, and intragenerational abuse are likely to be very different from each other. Some boys have endured several types of abuse, either simultaneously or successively. Before continuing with a detailed description of each one, let me briefly define the terms I use.

Intrafamilial abuse takes place inside the home of the child or adolescent. It is logical to include here not only sexual relations between father and son but also those between grandfather and grandson, between uncle and nephew, between brothers, between cousins, between stepfather and son by adoption, and between substitute father and child placed in a foster home. Nineteen respondents, that is almost two-thirds, had suffered at least one type of sexual aggression within their family.

Extrafamilial abuse, on the other hand, takes place outside the family nucleus. The abuser may be a friend, an aquaintance, or a neighbour of the family. Occasionally the abuser may even be someone completely unknown to the young person. Thirteen respondents had been sexually abused by a person outside their family or unknown to the family milieu.

Intergenerational abuse involves people belonging to different generations, i.e., where there is an age difference of at least fifteen years. In most cases, this means that sexual relations occur between a child or a young adolescent and an adult male. Twenty-four of the reported abuses come under this definition.

Intragenerational abuse takes place between boys who belong to the same generation, although the aggressor is older than his victim. It involves unwanted sexual relations between a child or young adolescent and an adolescent older than he is. Eleven respondents described such abuse.

The sketch below is made up of four quadrants. It illustrates the diversity of types of abuse experienced by the thirty respondents questioned. The numbers ascribed to each quadrant total more than thirty, since some boys had been subjected to several types of abuse.

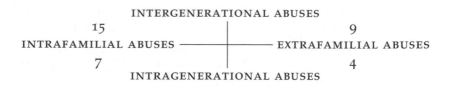

One could also categorize these different types of sexual abuse according to the dyads as follows:

INTERGENERATIONAL AND INTRAFAMILIAL ABUSES: Incest between father/son, stepfather/stepson, grandfather/grandson, uncle/nephew, substitute father/boy.

INTRAGENERATIONAL AND INTRAFAMILIAL ABUSES: Older brother or cousin/younger brother or cousin.

INTERGENERATIONAL AND EXTRAFAMILIAL ABUSES:	INTRAGENERATIONAL AND EXTRAFAMILIAL ABUSES:
Abuse committed by men who are not related to the boy: neighbour, park superintendent, father of a friend, friend of the family, stranger, etc.	Older adolescent/younger boy (not related).

DANGER IN THE HOME

Intergenerational abuse that is intrafamilial in nature involves a father, a stepfather, an uncle, a grandfather, a substitute father (as in a foster home), or the mother's male lover. In all cases under this grouping, the aggressor was at least fifteen years older than his victim. More far-reaching than this difference in age, and therefore in size and strength, however, was the authority the adult held over the child and the way that authority facilitated the abuse and made its disclosure difficult for the victim. Indeed, not only do the protagonists in this drama form part of the same family and live, either from time to time or permanently, under the same roof but the young boy generally lives in a situation where he is dependent upon the aggressor, which only serves greatly to amplify his confusion, whether the abuse continues or whether it is denounced. Respondents who faced the permanent threat in which this proximity placed them seem to have been the most devastated. Even where the abuse was denounced, the boy's anguish continued for fear of the family environment becoming disrupted.

This type of abuse truly depicts danger in the home (*Péril en la demeure*, to borrow the title of a French film). Such constant danger compounds the after-effects of the abuse, removing the security in the home that is essential to a child's development. Many victims have spoken graphically of the hell they have lived through, likening themselves to mice caught in a trap. It is not surprising that such victims form an early dependence on drugs, or a tendency towards self-mutilation or suicide: they are either seeking ways of escape or crying out for help.

Father-son incest turns a child's way of imagining the world upside-down. It results in a loss of the identity references a normal family provides and leaves the child questioning what he ought to be able to take for granted. Am I a man? Am I okay, normal? Who is my father? What is our relationship? Who am I in this family? Why does my father love me like that? Is my father my father, my worst enemy, my lover? Should I obey him? Why doesn't my mother protect me? Why do the other adults who know about it – if such is the case – do nothing about it?

Father-son sexual abuse breaks the double taboo of incest and homosexuality. This explains why it was for a long time the least reported of all forms of sexual abuse, despite its prevalence. Intergenerational and intrafamilial abuse was at one time so narrowly associated with father-daughter incest that even contemporary writers went so far as to affirm that father-son incest was rare, if not exceptional. Although the limited sample of this study is not necessarily representative, this is the form of abuse that appears to be the most common.

It is characteristic, indeed symptomatic, that all the fathers who were reported to have committed incest already had poor relationships with their sons, according to the sons' descriptions. All the boy victims of incest mentioned that their fathers were habitually absent, cold, authoritarian, or violent. These incestuous fathers had all mastered the distancing of which Boris Cyrulknik speaks when he remarks that attachment inhibits incest.[9] Studies of father-daughter incest have shown that a father's preoccupation with the well-being of his child greatly diminishes the risk of sexual molestation.[10] This finding is confirmed in cases of father-son incest. Fathers who have had little contact with their sons, or who have established distance, as Cyrulnik emphasizes, are more likely to disregard the incest taboo. In certain cases, ironically, it seems that sexualizing their relationship with a son was the only way for these men to "get close to" the child.

Several of the victims of father-son incest related that the preliminaries to or the moments following sexual contact with their fathers constituted the only occasions on which the latter had been at all attentive or affectionate towards them. Even where the boys considered that the price for this attention was high, most of them had hoped, however vainly, that it would lead to better communication with their fathers. Some gave in to this form of violence in order to prevent what they saw as worse punishments, or to avoid being grounded, deprived of money and food, or beaten if they did not cooperate; often those who gave in to the guilty wishes of their father were beaten just the same. By not resisting they could at least hope that the abusing man, once satisfied, would be more understanding – or at least would leave them alone for a while.

Seventeen-year-old Francis, who had been molested from the age of twelve, said: "My father told me that I excited him and that it was my fault if he wanted to have sex with me. He said that if I did not give him what he wanted, he would go after my little sister or leave my mother who didn't give him enough cunt." In the case of twenty-five-year-old Bruno, abused since he was six: "If I didn't go along [with his father's attentions], he would threaten never to buy anything else for me, give me money for school, or let me go out. When I simply went along with it, I would always have a small gift in return, and then he would be nicer with me during the next few days. He'd let me be."

Maxim had been violated by his substitute father from the age of eight. "When I resisted, he beat me until I gave in. After he climaxed, he would get angry with me again, I don't really know why. Maybe because I didn't make love nicely with him; because I didn't like it and kept on telling him to stop."

"My father never gave me any money," said Robert, a victim of abuse from the age of thirteen. "My mother spent some time in a psychiatric hospital. I had no one to turn to. I began going with men when I was twelve or thirteen, just to get attention and treats. My father somehow became aware of it. One day when I was in the shower, he came to join me, naked. Surprised, I struggled. He said to me, 'What? You don't want to do with your father what you do with the others? I'll reward you, too, if you're nice to me.' I was trapped. He must have followed me if he knew what was going on. From that moment, I had no choice."

Jimmy was seven the first time his father approached him sexually. "My father starts touching me, masturbating me. I don't understand what's happening and I don't try to understand. He says to me: 'Don't tell your mother, I'm not doing anything wrong.' I'm afraid but it's the only time he's gentle and affectionate towards me. It was like he had to get sex in order to show me affection."

Several of the respondents told me they had believed all boys went through the same thing and never spoke about it; in other words, that all adults wanted to have sex with children and were allowed to use them. In some cases the idea was supported by the fact that there were indeed several adults interested in them sexually. Justin, abused as a child by his father, an uncle, and then an older brother, could only deduce that "it's part of life." Paul, abused by his father, two of his brothers, and one of his sisters, then by strangers who gave him rides when he was running away, arrived at the same conclusion. How could he think otherwise? For Eric, who was sexually exploited by a foster father, then by the man's friends, and finally by the social work educators to whom he was entrusted, the situation became routine. An abandoned child, he had no choice but to submit to it. Now in his early twenties, he has so thoroughly absorbed the notion of "tit-for-tat" integral to the abuse he sustained that he has become a full-time prostitute.

In numerous cases, the adult did everything possible to make the commission of incest appear normal. The more a child hesitates to denounce abuse, the closer he comes to justifying it. Andrew quickly understood that sexually his father expected him to replace his mother. It was the same for Bruno and Robert, whose mothers were invalids: they told themselves that this explained and even justified the behaviour of fathers who were "deprived of sex and affection." Sometimes a child will try to rationalize the behaviour of a parent. Charles, induced by his father to have sexual relations with him, believed that at the time his father was depressed, tormented by the abuse he himself had no doubt suffered. Justin, a victim of incest from the age of four or five whose father was subsequently hospitalized on a psychiatric ward, thinks more or less the same thing.

Some boys, on the other hand, find it hard to rationalize incest to themselves. Harold's father made a habit of taking off the boy's clothes and then beating him, apparently with the intention of sexually exciting himself: "I know that it excited him ... It was not only physical abuse, it was also sexual abuse. I felt his penis through his trousers. I learned much later from my mother that my father had been beaten, undressed, in front of all the children at school when he was young. This had scarred him, probably. He took pleasure in doing the same thing to me, undressing me and spanking my buttocks. Beating me was like an excuse to humiliate me."

Jimmy and Francis, both abused over a period of years by violent fathers, declared that while they would like to come to understand and love their fathers, it seemed impossible as long as their fathers refused, completely in one case and partially in the other, to admit to what had happened and stop blaming their sons for having spoken out.

In addition to father-son incest, intergenerational/intrafamilial abuse consists of abuse committed by an uncle, a grandfather, or by the mother's lover. In all such cases, the respondents' families met disclosure of the abuse with astonishment, disbelief, and amazement, as though finding an aggressor among them was unthinkable. The grandfather of Frederic could certainly not be implicated. How could anyone suggest that a man so highly respected had obliged his little five-year-old grandson to perform fellatio on him? Worse still, how could anyone possibly believe he had subjected the majority of his grandchildren to the same thing? In the same vein, the "model" uncle, so attentive to Justin and Jean-Philippe, could not possibly have done what they claimed he had done. Similarly, the "big-hearted" foster fathers who took Maxim, Patrick, and Eric into their homes could not be the monsters these adolescents would describe years later. Not only is intrafamilial/intergenerational abuse among the most traumatising, it has proven without doubt to be the most denied and the most secret. This is not an understatement.

It has long been believed that sexual abuse within families usually involves girls, while third-party abuse is more likely to involve boys. This is a false belief. Although extrafamilial abuse of boys certainly does exist, such extrafamilial cases are not the only type of abuse of boys, nor are they, in all probability, the most frequent. Additionally, the closer the boy's relationship to the perpetrator, the more distressing, the more risky the abuse; hence the more improbable sounding when denounced and the more difficult the task of convincing other adults in the family of what is really going on. As one respondent, Jean-Philippe, said: "As kids we're told not to follow strangers, not to talk to men we don't know, etc. We're never told that the place where we are at most risk of being abused is at home, and that the person most likely to abuse us is someone we know well. As for warnings against paedophiles on the street and in parks or public toilets – don't make me laugh!"

WHEN LITTLE RED RIDING HOOD IS A BOY

The tale of Little Red Riding Hood can of course be read as an allegory. The wolf who intends to eat the little girl symbolizes the adult male who abuses her, having deceived her in order to gain her confidence. But now we see that Little Red Riding Hood can just as well be a boy – something the story did not tell us. Because little boys know how to defend themselves, it seems, no one can imagine that they too can be taken in by wolves.

Intergenerational/extrafamilial abuse is committed by people called third parties: neighbours, acquaintances of the family, or strangers. The victim and perpetrator may not be related in any way, but there is often a degree of affection between them. Such ties allow the aggressor to gain the trust of the child and subsequently procure the child's silence. So it was with Dennis, who was drawn into having sexual contact with the caretaker of the skating rink where he played hockey. So it was with Pascal, trapped by the only adult who seemed to be concerned about him. So also was it with Matthew, abused by the father of his best friend; Marcel, manipulated by an old neighbour with whom he had struck up a friendship; Jean-Paul, exploited by an acquaintance of his father; James, made use of by an adult who had picked him up when he had run away; Eric, handed over by his foster father as a prostitute to his colleagues from work; and Oliver, obliged to share his bed with his mother's lover. In all, nine of the men I interviewed had been victims of third-party abuse; of these, only one, Vladimir, had been abused by a stranger, a man who trespassed onto the school grounds where, at dusk, the young boy was still lingering.

Lonely boys, looking for affection or attention, are the preferred targets of third-party aggressors. Like incest victims, these boys have experienced difficult and strained father-son relationships. The adult who knows about spoiling and being affectionate often replaces, in the mind of the child, the father he does not have or with whom contact is nonexistent, cold, or very distant. Boy victims of abuse perpetrated by third parties are enormously vulnerable because they are desperately looking for an adult who will pay attention to them. Vladimir, for example, justifies the fact that he was dawdling in the school yard although it was quite late by saying: "I always went home as late as possible because I didn't want to see my dad. We couldn't stand one another." Father-son relationships that are difficult will incite some boys to approach other adults in the hope of finding the attention they cannot find at home. An unstable or non-supportive home environment can predispose a boy to be open to anything that looks like tenderness, no matter who is offering it. The boy's manner may also suggest to an aggressor that he is likely to be submissive and will, up to a point, "participate" in being abused, if only to the extent that he will not denounce it. To maintain a relationship that is somewhat rewarding, such a boy may be ready to bend to many require-ments until such time as the pressures and demands of the adult become so excessive that they render the relationship unbearable.

The loss of trust that follows will only further isolate a boy who has been subjected to such trickery. Matthew, abused by the father of his best friend when he was fourteen, today sees all men as potential rapists. His mistrust is extreme. Jean-Paul, sixteen today, regrets having accepted some years ago to "give pleasure" to a handicapped friend of his father who had known how to elicit his compassion. "He told me he would never be able to have a woman, that I was his only hope of finding a little affection. He really took me in!." As for James, he learned fast that the adult who took him into his house would not keep him very long if he refused to pay him "in kind."

Little Red Riding Hoods pay dearly for their naïveté. These boys experience, through their molestation, one more betrayal and one more abandonment. The man they believed would love them, in the broadest and most noble sense of the word, has exploited their deep need and their eagerness for affection. How can one possibly trust any other adult after that?

LIKE A BROTHER, LIKE A LOVER

I have borrowed the title of this section from an essay by Georges Michel Sarotte on homosexuality in American literature.[11] Intragenerational and intrafamilial abuse, that is, abuse between brothers or between cousins, is without doubt more frequent than we believe. Numerous aggressors have begun their activities within their own family by going after their younger brothers. Seven respondents have experienced this type of abuse: five with an older brother, and two others with a cousin or with a young uncle. In all the cases of incest between brothers, both were living under the same roof, sleeping in the same room, even in the same bed. When visiting, the aggressor cousin often shared the games and sometimes the bed of the child he abused. The uncle was the boy's guardian. The main difference between this and the other forms of incest is that here the instigator is relatively close in age to his victim, usually only a few years older, the victim being a child or young adolescent and the aggressor an older adolescent or young adult.

Paul, today aged twenty-eight, tells how two of his brothers and later an older sister abused him. The abuse began when he was five and continued until he was twenty-four, when he left home to go into a detox program, having become addicted in the years between. Pierre, now forty-four, had sexual relations with his older brother for seven years until he turned fourteen, when his brother left the house to get married. Joseph, now thirty, had frequent sexual relations with his brother from age eight to age eleven, the brother being between sixteen and nineteen years old at the time. These activities stopped for him too when the brother left to set up house. When he was an adolescent, Jean-Sylvain, thirty today, was expected to fill the sexual needs of a brother who was five years his senior. Jean-Marc, sixteen, was sexually abused by a cousin slightly older than himself when he was seven. Oliver was obliged to satisfy the young uncle, aged twelve, who was babysitting him. Justin, now thirty-four and a father himself, had repented sexual relations with his father, his uncle, and his brother, but it was with the latter that the relationship lasted longest, from the time Justin was thirteen until he reached sixteen. This brother was four years older than Justin and the relationship did not end until the eve of the older brother's wedding.

As this last case points out, situations of multiple sexual abuse are not exceptional, especially when members of the same family are implicated, as though a family subculture exists that encourages the reproduction of sexual aggression again and again. Thus, Paul was sodomized at the age of five by his father, then frequently molested by his two brothers. He learned to see himself as the sexual plaything of the others, who otherwise ignored him. As a young adolescent he tried several times to run away from home, but his attempts to escape these abuses led to his discovering the world of prostitution. He had so completely accepted the framework of abuse that it seemed to him normal.

With Pierre and Joseph, the relationships of bribery and mutual dependence established with their brothers culminated in depression for the one and refuge in drugs for the other. Neither believed they could escape the abuse. The memory of it continued to haunt them long after it had ended. Pierre, who has adopted a homosexual orientation, reports that he still sometimes dreams that he sees the head of his brother on the body of one of his lovers. For Jean-Sylvain, things seem less tragic since he was coerced less forcefully: he had the sense that he learned about sexuality with his brother, even if the latter's homophobic (and defensive) invective contrasts strongly today with Jean-Sylvain's avowed homosexuality: "It was my brother who taught me about the homosexuality for which he reproaches me today, as if he no longer remembers anything about what went on; as if it were not he who pushed me into it by making me explore a man's body and what one can do with it."

All these men have been marked by their sexual experiences with their brothers. Some admit, not without confusion, that they are still attracted to men who resemble the brothers they came to detest. When they develop an attraction for people of their own sex, men who have been forced to have sexual relations with one of their brothers see a correlation between their former incestuous experiences and their homosexual leanings. From this stems a certain guilt. They find it difficult to accept that their homosexual attractions could be the result of the sexual experimentation forced upon them by a brother they now condemn.

Incest between brothers is no easier to disclose than father-son incest. In none of the cases in this study did the parents believe the younger child when he was accusing one of his older brothers. One man had quite simply decided to remain silent for fear that the shock of such a revelation would kill his father or his mother. Some parents refused to listen to an accusing son because the perpetrator of the abuse was their favourite, or because the sibling who denounced him had in the meantime affirmed his homosexuality. Thus the homosexual child is suspected of having seduced his older, heterosexual brother. These older brothers are all in fact married, more or less happily, and have had children, something that their younger brothers worry about but tend to avoid dealing with. Oliver's experience, although it took place with a young uncle, is akin to these cases of incest between brothers. The case of Jean-Marc, abused at the age of seven years by a cousin, is a little different, since he did not hesitate to denounce the cousin when his threats and demands became intolerable. But the cost,

once again, was a family crisis: the parents of the one no longer
speak to the parents of the other whereas before they were the
closest of friends – something that only makes Jean-Marc feel
more guilty.

THE LAW OF THE JUNGLE

Cases of intragenerational and extrafamilial abuse were the rarest
among my study sample. They are perpetrated by older friends,
acquaintances, or neighbours who are themselves minors, that is
to say, adolescents, when the abuse first takes place. In this type
of abuse, perpetrator and victim have no family tie and there are
fewer than fifteen years between them in age, generally much less.
The stories of four respondents conform to this picture.

Martin, age sixteen, gave in to the desires of older friends he
had known in a group home and who had induced him to run
away with them. He was about twelve when he found himself in
bed with his benefactors to "thank" them. Steve, on the other
hand, was inveigled by older neighbours he hardly knew, having
just moved to their part of town, into joining them in a new game.
These adolescents undressed him and obliged him to perform
fellatio on them. Steve was five years old at the time. Now twenty-
five, he has AIDS contracted during his adolescence when he got
into prostitution. Antoine, seven years old at the time, was
involved with a sixteen-year-old neighbour. They often played
together. When the older boy's mother was absent, he would take
Antoine into his room and ask the child to masturbate him. Later
on it was fellatio, then anal intercourse. It was then that Antoine
refused to continue and told his parents everything. Some time
later, he himself initiated similar activities with a younger neighbour. Lastly, Serge was accustomed to playing in a wooded area
behind his parents' house when he was seven or eight years old.
An adolescent who was building a cabin in the woods offered to
help him do the same. They struck up a friendship and the older
boy led Serge into sexual activities that became more and more
overt. Serge finally told his parents, and then the police. The
police, however, took no steps to restrain the young aggressor.

It is surprising to find out that in many cases (one in three, in
this research) the perpetrator was another young person, although
a little older and belonging to the victim's group of brothers or

circle of friends. Child molesters often begin their careers very early. As soon as they feel they can be the stronger one, certain boys (but not all – a point that I discuss in another chapter) who have been victimized physically or sexually will try to replay the same traumatic scenario, this time reversing the roles. Before recognizing that they have a problem, and before others recognize that they have a problem, replaying their abuse seems to them to be a resolution. I shall come back to this important matter.

In sum, the more closely related the aggressor is to the child, the more intrusive and threatening their relationship will seem to the victim. For the same reasons, the victim will be more uncomfortable about running away from or denouncing the situation. It also seems that the younger the abused child, the likelier that he will be abused several times or by more than one aggressor. Such trauma can leave scars that cannot be erased. An accumulation of physical, psychological, and sexual abuse by a father is particularly insidious since one form of abuse can include but also conceal another. Those who work with young people must be more aware of this. All types of abuse, however, have a negative impact on the victim, as the life stories presented throughout this work demonstrate only too well.

JIMMY'S STORY

Jimmy, sixteen, was a victim of father-son incest from the age of seven to thirteen.

I was always rejected by my father because I wasn't how he wanted me to be. I had problems at school because of that. I was supersensitive and cried all the time if the other kids picked on me, or if things just didn't go right. The other boys laughed at me because of this. They called me names. My father wasn't proud of me; he didn't talk to me. The only place I could be alone at home was in my own room. My dad didn't allow me to watch TV: he said I hadn't earned it. He was really strict and his rules were rigid. I was reprimanded for being the slightest bit late. To punish me, he took away my toys. I played with my socks instead. I pretended they were animals, trucks, people. My mother acted as a go-between. She tried to prevent my being punished or hit but she avoided contradicting him, so he wouldn't turn on her perhaps.

As a child I was unhappy. I looked at the fathers of my friends and wondered if mine was normal. He never played with me, never did sports with me. People think an only child is spoiled. Well, it wasn't true for me. My grandparents spoiled me from time to time. My parents didn't have much money, and they didn't give me very much. Maybe they regretted having me. Then again, my father really had it in for his parents because they hadn't paid for his education, so maybe it pissed him off to see them spoiling me.

I had trouble getting along with other kids. I was jealous of them, with their great toys and the attention they got from their parents. I missed out on all that. I tried to understand my father's money problems, but it didn't change anything.

The first time it happened, I had just turned seven. One evening, my father came into my room with a flashlight. He came close, sat down on my bed, and started touching me. I mean abusing me. I didn't understand and I didn't try to understand what was going on. Right then, I thought it was part of a game, that all children did this. He fondled me, he lay down and rubbed himself against me. He said not to tell my mother about it. He said he wasn't doing it to be wicked. I didn't trust my father after he asked me to lie.

I didn't know too much about sex. I was never taught anything about it. I didn't know how to react. I obeyed my father. My mother never suspected anything. It wasn't really regular, just once in a while. He'd ask me to go to his room when my mother wasn't there, right up until I was about thirteen. It was about once a month. I didn't count how often.

I didn't like him touching me but those were the only times he took any notice of me unless he was punishing me. After he came, he'd light a cigarette, talk to me, ask me questions – he'd ask why it wasn't going well at school, or at home. We'd roughhouse on the bed like two friends: for once he was nice. It was as though I had to allow myself to be abused to be worth talking to. As soon as he got out of bed, he was the same as before. He treated me like an object, a thing. I was his thing.

Towards the end, when I began to refuse, he said to me: "Don't expect me to be nice with you in future." I started asking myself questions when I had my first girlfriend. I was finding it difficult to have a girlfriend while continuing to have sex with my father. I had understood what my father was doing. From that time on, I tried to resist him. He would begin to fondle me but I would say no. Faced with my lack of cooperation, he finally left me alone.

When I was little, each time I did the smallest thing wrong, I knew my father would beat me or punish me. I used to cry at the sight of him, right up until I was a teenager. Later I became aggressive towards him. My mother told me to settle things with him myself, that I was big enough. So the next time he tried to hit me, I stood up to him and defied him: "Go on! Hit me!" He walked off and didn't touch me. Before, I used to throw myself on the floor when he hit me. Now I was standing up to him, as if I wasn't afraid of him any more. He was a man who could be violent and kick me in the ribs, throw things at me, hit me with his fists. As soon as I felt stronger, more confident, I began to be less respectful towards him, to yell and scream my head off as he used to do. I saw my father as the enemy, as my worst enemy. He said: "Obey me. I'm your father." I replied: "A father doesn't behave the way you do."

The first time I kissed my first girlfriend I was embarrassed.
I was wondering about my father. Why does he do that?
Between my girlfriend and my father – how is it different?
What does my father mean to me? At that age you begin to
hear about homosexuals. I said to myself I was not homosexual, that I went out with girls. But my father … Why does he
do that? On the other hand, he's not gay … I realized that my
friends didn't have this kind of relationship with their fathers,
that they didn't have the problems I had.

During all those years I never spoke about what was happening. No one knew about it. When there was talk about love or
about sex at school, I was embarrassed. I really had no experience of that. I knew very little about girls. I had my first sexual
encounters with girls at fourteen or fifteen. When I was making
love, I tried not to think of my father, but interfering images
constantly came to me. I found myself to be awkward sexually
and it upset me not to know how to go about it. The fact that
I had finally been able to refuse my father reassured me. Today,
in my encounters with girls I'm the one who makes the deci-
sions. They have to go along with me, not force me. I prefer
girls who are more passive because they must take me as I am.
I'm not easy, I'm often argumentative. If I go without having
a girl for a while, it worries me. I ask myself if I'll be able to
find another.

As for guys, I don't trust them. I was friends with this
twenty-four-year-old guy who worked in the foster home I was
placed in after the incest was disclosed. I got very attached to
him. He was like a substitute father. He invited me to his place
to look at films, do whatever I liked. He taught me music, took
me out. I was fourteen. He had become my best friend. Then
I discovered he was gay. I had noticed that he only invited guys
to his place. Even though he hadn't done anything bad with
me, this discovery set off an alarm inside me. I stopped talking
to him and made fun of him with my friends. I broke off all
contact with him. Today, if a homosexual approaches me he's
likely to lose a few teeth …

I myself have trouble understanding who I am. I've become
intolerant and weepy; I have an unstable personality. I find I'm
quite isolated. Taking drugs hasn't helped. I tell myself I've
become like my father. That really disheartens me.

After I was sent to the group home, I decided to disclose my
incest in order not to become a perpetrator myself. I found
myself there because I was stealing from shops. I was doing it
for the risk, for the challenge, for the mixture of fear and pleasure. Once at the group home, I spilled the beans. I decided to
take my father to court for what he had done. I was hesitant,
but my social worker encouraged me and arranged for me
to meet with a lawyer. I told myself it was good for me and
it would help my father too. I made a declaration where
I recounted everything. They arrested my father. He owned up.
Today he is on probation.

I haven't seen my father again. I didn't have to testify
because he pleaded guilty. I've had no news of him since then,
only from my mother. My relationship with her became very
cold for several months. My father worked her up against me,
but then she was mad at me for my drug habit too. As for her,
she wants to help my father. She minimizes the seriousness of
what he's done. The other day, on the telephone, she said to
me: "Anyway, it's not like he abused ten people; you were the
only one." That hurt me, hearing that. As if what I had gone
through didn't count. When I told her what had been going on,
she told me she had suspected something without knowing
exactly what. She didn't know whether to believe me. The more
time passed, the less she believed me, because of my behaviour
problems. I don't find it right, what she's doing. She tells me
stupid things, tries to blame me, to make me believe that it's
my fault, what happened. The last time we talked, I overdosed
on mescaline the next day.

My father is afraid of going to jail. He has bad memories of
the one night he spent there. His relationship with my mother
has changed. He no longer has that strong man image. Now it's
my mother who wears the trousers. As for me, I'm quite lost in
all of this and just want to cry when I think about it. I wonder
whether I could love my father in spite of everything. I have to
force myself to say I don't love him. And I feel guilty myself.
Do I love him? Do I not love him? It's hard to figure out.

The longer this goes on the more depressed I get. Who am I?
I don't know. I dont know why it happened, either. If my father
hadn't abused me I wouldn't be here, in a group home. I would
be sitting at home, I'd be okay. Basically, all the problems I've

had are due to him, to what he did to me. I don't accept it.
I lost my childhood because of him. Now I'm losing my adolescence. Will I lose my whole life like that? I might just as well
finish it right now.

But there is something positive in my life right now. I'm
learning music, and I'm writing poetry and songs. I have
projects with my friends. I'd like to study music or literature.
I'm getting ahead little by little. It's encouraging to see that
people find me talented. I ask myself whether they mean it.

Children? No, I don't want any. I don't want to get married
either: it's not worth it. My parents haven't exactly been a good
example. I would like to have a girlfriend, but children, no.
I don't want a complicated life. I would like to be wealthy, to
be free of problems, live on my own mountain, be able to watch
the people down below without them being able to hurt me.
The worst thing for a guy who's been abused is confusion,
mixed with fear of what's going to happen; that's on top of the
despondency and low morale. Even your reasoning is no longer
what it should be. Sometimes I don't understand what people
are trying to say to me. I don't understand what they are
doing ...

I put on a tough front. People think I'm hard but I'm just
acting a role, like in a drama. I identify to a great extent with
Jim Morrison of The Doors. I would love to make music and
write like him. The essential is that I will have to be myself. But
it's as though I no longer have an identity, that I'll have to glue
one on, so to speak. I do have a made-up identity, but it's only
a role I play. It's hard for boys like me to find out who they
really are. I identify with Jim Morrison because I sense he went
through the same thing I did. His behaviour, his problems with
his father, and his mother too, it makes me think of someone
who has suffered incest. He was turned inward on himself,
and he wrote, like I do. We have a lot in common. He bore
an image: The Lizard King. As for me, I bear the image of
an image.

ERIC'S STORY

Eric, twenty-three years old, was abused from the time he was six by the father of the foster family that took him in. He was subsequently abused by the friends of this man, as well as by a social service educator.

When I was first placed in a foster home, I was very young. I don't remember my mother. She was like a cat in heat, like a bitch. She gave birth to babies just to abandon them. It's okay if I don't know anything about her; I hate her anyway. She gave birth to me just to make me miserable. My father didn't do any better. I don't know him either and I don't want to know him.

The abuse began in the foster family where I grew up. It began when I was about six. The husband made love to me when his wife wasn't home. He said I had a beautiful penis for my age, that I did it well ... Sometimes, he brought friends home from work. I had to do the same things with them. They gave me little gifts in return. At one point I stopped being mad about it. I was only doing what they wanted, so they wouldn't scold me or punish me. I was trying not to think about it too much. After a while, you learn to live with it.

When the social workers began to suspect what was going on, they moved me to a group home. I was almost twelve. I was used to making love with men and it probably showed, I don't know. There was an educator who always had his eye on me. I could feel it. Most of the time nothing much happened, but sometimes, yes, it went further. He gave me special privileges in return. I kept quiet. I told myself all men are the same: just interested in butt.

Maybe I even got to enjoy it. The only time anyone paid attention to me was when I had sex with them. You learn fast. But I'm not gay. I don't think I am. I like women too much for that. If I haven't ever done very much with them, it's because of embarrassment – lack of opportunity mostly. Then again, I won't start looking for a girl right now; I would seem too stupidly naive.

Once I ran away from the group home and I met a girl. We ended up in a motel, by pooling the money we had. I jumped into bed with that girl. It was the first time. I was quite

nervous. I had taken drugs. I wanted so much for it to work
that it didn't work. I was disappointed, the girl too. I tried
another time but it just didn't click any better. I didn't go out
with girls after that.

When I left the group home, I didn't have a trade and
I didn't know where to go. I ended up meeting a guy who took
me to live with him. I didn't work. I paid him my share "in
kind," until we no longer got along. I found myself in the street
again and became a prostitute. It was all I knew – the only
trade I ever learned. I've been making love with men since
I was six years old.

In that area, things have always gone well. Sometimes I meet
a man who likes me enough to look after me for a while, so
that I don't have to get into prostitution. Other times, I don't
have the choice: I have to make money, do my bit. I cruise
seven nights out of seven. I haven't counted, but I must have
gone through several hundred men in five years. I have a sort
of clientele. I always walk the same beat. The johns trust me.
They know I'm clean, I'm not a rotten type and they'll get their
money's worth.

While I was living with a photographer I did erotic photo-
graphy. It makes me laugh to see myself in magazines from
time to time. Once, when I found myself in a jam, I danced
nude in a gay bar. But it was too much for me. I couldn't take
everyone trying to touch me. I have my self-respect. I'm not
an object.

I've been quite sick lately. Maybe I've got AIDS. But I keep
going; I don't want to know. Life's not worth living in any case.
I get by on coke. Impossible to do otherwise. Sucking cocks is
not very interesting. It's better when there's a certain affection.
I keep on telling myself that one day, I'll find someone who will
look after me without having to be involved sexually. Men,
once they've had what they want, they get tired of you.

I was a good kid before – before I got disgusted with everyone, disgusted with living. I couldn't seem to escape from it.
There was always someone to put me back in the shit.

When I get up, about noon, it's like a reflex. I get ready, I go
looking for clients. If I'm lucky, I can find two or three in the
same day. I never have enough money. There's never any left.
I've tried to have my own apartment but it was too complicated.

That's why I move from one place to another. I don't have a fixed adress.

When I went before the judge to testify against the guy who abused me, the lawyers said I was lying. I gave them a bit of lip, told them to fuck off. I was thrown out of court. The accused is probably laughing. He got a ridiculously light sentence and was out almost immediately. There's no justice in this world. Us, young people, we're nothing.

I'm telling you this because you're conducting research on the subject. I'll be dead maybe by the time you've finished it. I have no family, no one to count on. When I die it won't make any difference to anyone. But you can tell the world that I would have liked it, me too, to have a real family, to be loved for real, not just for my butt. Today, I can't even say I'm abused. It's rather me that chases after men. If I do have AIDS and if I can pass it on to some of them, there won't be so many of them around exploiting young people.

CHAPTER THREE

Vulnerable and Trapped:
How Sexual Abuse Comes About

The circumstances surrounding the childhood abuse of the young men interviewed for this study show how trapped they were in one way or another. Most of the boys were profoundly vulnerable, both physically, as children, and psychologically, as lonely, rejected, or unloved youngsters with troubled families. That is why so many of them, at least at the beginning, saw their relationship with the aggressor as a last hope or refuge. The aggressor could be an uncle who takes the place of an absent, indifferent, or violent father; the brother who pays a certain amount of attention to a younger sibling who is neglected by the rest of the family, or the friend who shows himself available at a time when the young boy has a special need. The aggressor could also be a father who is at last showing some interest in his son.

The men who agreed to tell their stories for this study come from all social classes and all milieux. It is clear that sexual abuse of boys is widespread: it is present in the city and the country, in well-to-do families as well as in underprivileged ones. The aggressors – farmers, soldiers, educators, security guards, merchants, doctors, policemen, manual labourers, etc. – represent all types of employment. Another important point is that most of them are described by their victims as being avowedly heterosexual, sometimes bisexual, very rarely homosexual. Evidently, erotic attraction towards children transcends sexual orientation and bears no relation to the categories generally used to denote attraction towards adult males or females. Moreover, sexuality is not the only factor to be considered. The context in which the relationship takes place is complex, sometimes ambiguous, and, for the respondents (as for us), difficult to comprehend.

As already noted, it is often the case that the father of the abused child is absent, indifferent, or violent. The boy feels the absence in his life of a masculine figure who is attentive and gratifying, and this the aggressor can profit from (even where the father is the aggressor). Peter, who was seen as the lame duck of the family, was happy that one of his brothers seemed somewhat interested in him. Matthew, abandoned by his father, was proud that the father of his best friend took care of him as though he were his own son. Marcel received from a neighbour who could have been his grandfather the affection he lacked at home. Jimmy and Francis at last saw their fathers giving them some of their time, after they had satisfied them sexually. James thought himself lucky to find someone who took him in when he was a runaway. Serge had found a big brother in the adolescent who taught him how to build a cabin in the woods. And so on. Except in the rare case of rape by an unknown person the aggressor will often try to assume the role of a significant adult in the child's life, the better to snare him later.

Most of the boys who were molested were driven by an intense quest for affection. In some cases the children perceived both parents, not just their father, as indifferent, distant, or "rejecting." Some boys went so far as to say they would have done anything at all just to be loved. One can imagine that they were easy to take advantage of, including by their fathers or others who may have been responsible for the child's actual circumstances. In short, when the man preparing to molest him begins to show interest in a child or adolescent, the boy is all the more available and receptive, so great is his need for affection. The abuse itself is sometimes accepted in silence because the boy feels attached, in a certain sense, to the older person who has found a way to exploit his affection for his own ends.

Most respondents are now aware that their aggressors played on their ingenuousness and vulnerability. One young person, who was molested by several men at different points in his life, puts it this way: "You might say they sense it in us: 'I am vulnerable, I have already been abused,' as though it's written on our foreheads." Maxim, Eric, Justin, Oliver, and Paul, who have all been violated by more than one person, imagine that something in them attracted that type of exploiter. How? They do not know exactly. Some believe it was the softness of their bodies, their refined features, or their fairness. Others think that when they were children or adolescents, there was something feminine about them that could excite and lead men on (as if the abuse of these boys could only have happened because of mistaken gender. I return to this question later).

According to Conte, Wolf, and Smith,[1] child abusers themselves say they are able to recognize vulnerable children who would be easy to abuse. They are isolated, pushed aside by their families, uncomfortable with themselves, in need of gratification. Aggressors who wish to take advantage of such a situation will gradually accustom the targeted child to increasing physical contact, beginning with nonsexual parts of the body before progressing to the genital area. This progressive contact is orchestrated in such a way that the child feels that he was willing. He dit not say no, for example, when the adult massaged his back. Sexual abuse is less an act or a group of acts than a gradual process, a series of gestures leading up to what is intolerable for the entrapped youngster.

The child's troubled family situation makes him not only more vulnerable to abuse but all the more receptive to its rules: a conspiracy of silence, emotional and sometimes financial blackmail, the resulting give-and-take agreement (the man gives attention or money and the young person gives his sexuality). The more dysfunctional the family, the more prepared the boy seems to do or to submit to whatever is asked of him. He behaves this way in order to be "chosen" by someone who will be nice to him in some way. Most of the respondents, before their aggressors disclosed their real intentions, were hopeful of finding the caring relationship they had never had, or no longer had, which explains why they offered so little resistance, at least in the beginning. The reporting in this regard is significant. Paul, abused by different members of his family and later by strangers who gave him lifts when he was hitch-hiking, confides: "I was so desperate for affection that I would have said yes to anyone just to have a little attention."

Charles relates: "When my father began caressing me, masturbating me, I was flabbergasted. You certainly are surprised when this happens to you. You ask yourself what it's all about. But I was ambivalent. I knew it wasn't right, but at the same time I was happy that he was looking after me, that he was showing me affection by doing that. And I have to admit, it was then that I got to know my body and sexual pleasures."

Marcel, one of the youngest respondents in this study, relates: "My mother was a call-girl. It didn't last long between her and my father. They got divorced when I was about three years old. My father got remarried. He asked for custody. He got it but he never showed affection towards me, never took me in his arms like parents normally do. Neither did my stepmother. When they had children together, I saw all too well that they did love *them*. It was this affection that I never had, anywhere, that this certain man, an elderly neighbour, brought me. That's why I went along with it, without saying anything, even when my parents began to wonder if something was going on because I was always over there." Francis, forced to have sexual relations with his father when he was twelve, remembers: "It was the first time he paid attention to me, gave me affection, even if I considered it was not the best way."

Other respondents say practically the same thing. Does this mean that the men who took advantage of them did not know how to show affection except in a sexual way? Or was the affection merely an aid to exploiting the boy's naïvety? Whatever the truth is, many boys will accept a degree of sexualized affection because for them "it's either that or nothing." If they do not want to lose the attention of the adult who is offering this "affection," they must submit to his sexual desires. Of course, many end up rebelling against and refusing such an exchange, but they will all have conformed to its logic during a period of a few days, a few weeks, months, or even a few years of their life. One can even reflect that this sexualization of affection they have lived through will lead some of them to integrate this *modus vivendi* into their own life, something that will not be without consequences, as we shall see later on.

A boy who is assaulted sexually and who does not fight back has learned that if he is to receive affection and attention, he must pay with sex. The trap is closed before the child can protect himself against it, and before he has realized what is going on. Because of his young age, he does not even grasp the portent of the gestures he is expected to submit to. Above all, he does not perceive that it is only a beginning and that, if the relationship continues, the aggressor will in time make additional demands.

Inevitably he will be swept along on a tide of deception, disen-
chantment, and trauma. Some of the testimony is particularly
eloquent on this subject. "He made me go all the way. I'd like to
see him dead for having manipulated me," said Matthew of the
father of his best friend. "At the beginning he only pawed me, he
was nice to me in return," relates Jean-Marc, speaking of his
cousin, "but afterwards he always asked me to go further. I hesitate; I know it isn't right, but he threatens me: 'If you don't want
to, if you tell, my friends will break your neck.'" As for Marcel,
he remembers the first contacts he had with his elderly neighbour:

The first time he saw me, he asked me to do little jobs for him. Then, he
invited me to his home to watch videos. It was after two or three visits
that he took his clothes off. He undressed to his bare skin, saying "Touch
me." He undressed me too, masturbated me. He told me not to speak
about it. Deep down, I was happy that an adult would pay attention to
me, would take me in his arms, give me affection, tell me he loved me
– something my father had never done. Then I was thinking that everyone does this with children. It was my stepmother who found it strange
that I spent so much time with this man and who learned that he had
already abused other children. Right at that time, they began telling us
at school not to let anyone touch our body. I finally spoke up and told
my stepmother, but I didn't tell her everything. She forbade him to see
me and then she made a complaint to the police. It was after that I began
to ask myself questions, to find it bizarre, what we did, even if I continued to see him in secret before he went to prison. I was asking myself:
Is this normal? How can I make him stop? He had always been nice with
me. He gave me presents, loaned me his things. I wanted his affection
but without the sex. Not him. That's what I didn't like.

As this testimony demonstrates, it is precisely his emotional
involvement in the relationship that leaves the child confused and
hesitant. The emotional needs of the young person and the sexual
demands of the adult or older child are fundamentally incompatible. Some boys were well aware that something "not normal" was
going on. But what was it? They fervently hoped they were mistaken. Or else, after the first abuse, they imagined that things would
soon return to normal. Bruno, assaulted by his stepfather, said: "He
promised me not to do it again, but it would always begin again."
Matthew, aggressed by the father of his best friend: "He spoiled me
enormously, as much as if not more than his own son. My mother

was really suspicious. As for me, I didn't dare think of the worst [being abused]. I tried not to think of that." Maxim, violated on several occasions in his foster family, said: "I always hoped that this would be the last time, that he would finally let me alone when he had had enough." Finally, Patrick, already a victim of sexual abuse and subsequently caught up in the advances of a respected adult, said, "I had never been spoiled in my life. It was the first time that somebody loved me. I didn't know how to say no to him. I was afraid he would drop me afterwards. I told him I liked women, hoping he would at last understand."

By feigning affection or friendliness in a relationship whose real objective is to obtain sexual favours, the would-be aggressor leads the boy astray. Furthermore, he acts in such a way that the boy will eventually feel guilty for allowing himself to be fooled that way. It is only when the boy realizes he cannot extricate himself from the sexual relationship that he understands that he is trapped. The very attachments formed with the person who exploits his naïvety often prevent the child from revealing his secret. Perceiving the deal imposed upon them as a necessary evil, many boys will themselves come to give affection a sexual connotation and will finally accept more easily the sexual relationship with the aggressor.

If it is now relatively easy to understand how the relationship between the aggressor and the boy comes about, it is more difficult to grasp why the relationship persists after sexual abuse begins. It must be remembered that sexual abuse is most commonly part of a continuous process. Social worker Carol Hubberstey[2] divides the dynamics of sexual abuse into four phases:

1 Engagement of the young person by the adult or older child who will make use of him;
2 The abuse itself, sometimes perceived by the young person as payment for the attention and affection received;
3 The subsequent attempt by the young person to adapt to the situation, while at the same time asking himself how he can make the experience bearable or tolerable;
4 The outcome, that is, either the cessation of the abuse, if such is the case, or the evolution of the situation into something else, such as sexual abuse committed by the young person himself, an "escape" into drugs, into delinquency or into prostitution, etc.

From this one can conceive how the abused boy finds himself imprisoned in a cage whose mechanisms he does not grasp. It goes without saying that he must either try to extricate himself from the trap or accommodate himself to it.

This chapter has thrown some light on the first two elements of the dynamic described by Hubberstey: the initial gearing up of the relationship and the trap concealed within it. In following chapters we will spend some time examining how the young person perceives the abuse and the mechanisms put into effect to adapt to it, especially when the situation is not immediately denounced. We will look at how the young male victim of sexual abuse is susceptible to carrying over his traumatic experiences and his distress into his own life scenarios, including his emotional life, his love life and his sex life.

PHILIP'S STORY

Philip, twenty-eight, was abused by an uncle from the time he was nine until he turned sixteen.

The first big shock of my life was my mother's death when I was nine. I knew she was sick, but no one ever told me she might die. Until then nothing too bad had happened to me. The death of my mother shocked and depressed me. If she had still been alive, nothing would have happened as it did. After her death, my father became helpless and it was the children who had to parent him. He left for work very early in the morning and came home late at night. He never talked to us, never said nice things ... We knew he loved us but he never showed it, not in front of us, anyway. He loved us, but in silence. After my mother's death, he was wrapped up in himself, not really aware of what was going on around him.

The following summer, I stayed with an uncle, my mother's brother. He was fortyish. How did it happen? He used to fondle me when I went to bed, through my clothes. I wondered about it but not too much. I thought he was doing it to show affection. After a while, he went further. The first time he undressed me I knew something was wrong. But I wasn't strong enough to get free from him. He coaxed me: "You see, I love you, I'm showing you affection." Since I didn't get any affection anywhere else, I said nothing, I went along with it, but I felt guilty. Today I would think and I would act differently. At that point in time, I didn't even know what abuse was. Afterwards, he indulged me, gave me presents, took me on some nice outings. Maybe I was naive: it was like he was buying me. Today, I ask myself if I wasn't something of a prostitute since I received things in exchange for keeping quiet.

In the course of time, the sexual encounters became quite frequent: two or three times a week, whenever he had the chance. During this time I still got along quite well with him. He was my "gâteau" uncle (as they say in the French language), the only one in the family who paid me any attention. The sex was like something on the side, that I ought to give him in return. Then again, this abuse had introduced me to sensations I hadn't been aware of. Did I want it, did I not want it?

I was discovering the pleasure, the enjoyment. The question of homosexuality didn't even surface at that time. I had the impression that it was all quite normal. It was later, when my buddies began to have girlfriends, that I started asking myself questions. Since no one was talking about stuff like that, since my uncle was telling me it was our secret, that others didn't need to know about it, the situation continued until I no longer took my holidays with him, that is, until I was sixteen years old.

Still, it was pretty obvious that things weren't okay. Since my first summer with him, I started wetting my bed at night. I think that was the first consequence. It was almost as though I was afraid to be taken by surprise during the night: I lost control of myself. I was incontinent especially while I lived with my uncle. Then I became aggressive towards my brothers and sisters. For a few years, I admit, I didn't question what was going on, but when I was about twelve or thirteen I often thought about what was happening and wondered about it. I compared myself to others and realized I wasn't normal. When I might have wanted to talk about it, I figured that nobody else talks about anything, so why should I?

Around when I was twelve or so, when I started secondary school, I was looking at the boys in the shower. I imagined myself in bed with them. But I was ambivalent. I was looking at the girls too, even if my attraction towards men was more pronounced at that time. At some point I didn't want my uncle to touch me any more. He took me by force. He took me by the throat as if he wanted to strangle me, so that I wouldn't move. He threatened to grab my sister if I didn't shut my mouth. It became a constant fear for me – I didn't know he was already abusing her, something she only told me many years later.

I thought maybe I was encouraging him. Maybe something I did or the way I behaved was sending him signals. I told myself that, since no one was intervening, it was because I deserved it. I was more and more ashamed, and that's still with me today. I don't want to be with anyone, man or woman, who would want sex with me. When someone seems to be interested in me, I imagine it's just for sex. I would like to meet someone, but I can't get away from the idea of abuse, the fear of sexuality. I am not used to receiving pleasurable caresses. I feel bad when someone touches me. A person who touches

me disgusts me. And sperm, even my own, I find it disgusting.
I dont like kissing on the mouth, either. Everything he did to
me … today I don't like that.

All my relationships finish badly. Some years ago, I lived
with a girl and when it came time to sleep together I pushed
her away. I loved her, but I didn't like the feel of her body, her
kisses, her touching me. It was like being a prisoner. I went
through the same thing with a boy. With him, like with her,
I wanted their presence, but my way: I didn't want to have sex
with them. I enjoyed the attention they paid me, their tenderness, but I didn't really want to go further.

As an adolescent, I wasn't very comfortable with myself.
I was often alone. I was quick to anger also: I would swear at
my older sister, who looked after me, as if I wanted to get back
at her for having left me at the mercy of my uncle. I don't
really want to be ornery with people, but I am always on the
defensive. As soon as anyone does things for me, pays attention to me, I turn off. I must be the one in control of the relationship. When I risk losing control, I distance myself. I say to
myself, It's not possible that someone is interested in me unless
it's to make use of me. I am overly on guard.

During my high school years I attempted suicide. I saw my
friends happy, in love, whereas I was all alone. I began doing
drugs – coke. I was self-destructive. Maybe I was asking for
help that way. The day after my first attempt, I told my whole
story to one of my older brothers. He did nothing at all despite
his promise to confront my uncle. Worse, he continued to have
this uncle babysit his children as if there was nothing to it! I'm
still mad at him over this. He was the only one who could have
believed me, protected me, even if it was after the event.

It was only years later, after a second suicide attempt, that
I told the whole family what had been going on. I think they
were afraid they might actually lose me. Some of them became
closer, others distanced themselves from me. My four brothers
have also been abused by this uncle, even if they have never
openly said so. They didn't want to testify, they didn't want
it to be made known. They wanted me to keep silent so as
not to break up our uncle's marriage. I don't agree. I don't
want to harm anyone, but I don't want to bury myself by
being silent.

Why did it happen to me? I have been asking myself this question for a long time. After I knew that my sister and probably my brothers had been through the same thing, I told myself that it was my uncle's problem, because he went after anything that moved. I reproach him both for what happened but also for having forced me to live with it and keep it to myself. Today I can't have a normal relationship. Even if I am attracted to a man or a woman, I don't want to fantasize; I never masturbate. I'm attracted to well-built guys who make me feel protected. My uncle, he wasn't at all attractive. He was fat and dirty, and he smelled. I find this type of guy the most repulsive. I don't feel the same repugnance for women. But I don't want to be with just anybody. I am quite materialist from every point of view and I'm drawn to what is beautiful, as though, somehow, I want to savour the essence of things.

I don't like my body. Maybe its because I haven't appreciated the sexual relationships I've had. I'd like to have a different body, a complete makeover so I can say I'm starting my life over from zero. After all, the abuse went on right up to age sixteen: my body still looks somewhat the same and in my mind I can still feel his hands on me. I feel dirty. I'll never forget what has happened. And I can't live with these memories.

It's not silence that will help me free myself. Because of my past, I can't really manage to savour the beautiful things in life. With time I've begun to find some interest in living. I have a little more faith in myself, but I'm still afraid. Once, after a long holiday, I decided I was going to make something of my life. I have always been drawn to children. Not to abuse them for sure, but to work with them. But I was scared that, in the longer term, this attraction might become physical because of the abuse I've lived through. But it's the opposite that has happened. I chose to be close to children so that I could try to understand them, to protect them. I feel good about my work today as a teacher. When a child is living in an incestuous situation, I can talk to the child about it. This year I noticed that a little girl in my class was having problems. It made me feel better about myself to have been able to detect it and help guide her in the right direction. She's getting help now. I've finally realized that my fear of hurting children was unfounded. I have never been physically or sexually attracted like that.

It was a great relief to realize this about myself. It is often said that people who have been abused will abuse. It's not true, and it is dangerous to say things like that: it's probably one reason why so many male victims of abuse stay silent.

My abuser? I saw him recently but I don't look at him any more. At my grandfather's funeral, I didn't shake his hand, I walked right past him just as though he wasn't there. I pretend he doesn't exist, even though I know it's not the best solution. He has managed to avoid the consequences of his actions: nothing ever happens to him. Even though I spoke up about him, no one thought about going to court, or seeking justice.

I've been in therapy, but I was the only one talking. Faced with abuse situations, most social workers or psychologists don't know what to say. I had to help myself. In the hospital, after my second suicide attempt, I had to see a specialist. I was sleeping on the floor in the hospital: I had decided never to get into a bed because it's a place where we can be abused. I was sleeping in a corner, curled up in a ball, and I felt safe. It was one of my friends who had come to see me who rescued me. He took me in his arms and talked with me. I came back to reality. I sensed that he held me like that not because he wanted to abuse me but because he wanted to protect me. I felt I was important to him.

Ideally, I would like to find myself on my own in a place where everything is beautiful and pure, where everything that happens is agreed upon. There at least I could be with someone without risk. I am bisexual, perhaps, but I don't want sex. I lived for a little while with a girl, then with a boy. In the end I told them I was having sexual activities to please them. I needed some contact but not necessarily that kind of contact. I have given myself for so long without wanting it that I risked making a habit of it. I really have no need to experience sexual pleasure, but the need I have is for someone to love me.

I would like to make a family, have children one day, but I would never risk my children experiencing what I have lived through. Not that I would be afraid that I might commit the abuse myself, but I would always be afraid that someone else might. I am not dangerous. On the contrary, I am someone people confide in easily. I like people and I'm afraid of them, both at the same time.

Matthew, eighteen, was abused by the father of his best friend when he was fourteen.

I'm a pretty ordinary guy. Except that, when I feel threatened, I become violent. I can't control myself. It's as if a light goes on in my head and the words "self-defence" appear. When this happens I just go blindly ahead and I don't think of the consequences.

When I was little I tried to please everyone. I was very dependent; I needed a lot of attention. I lost both my fathers, one after the other. It was hard for me. First of all, I hardly knew my real father: he left when I was a baby. Then my mother remarried but that man left too when I was seven years old, because they got divorced. For me, that second man was my real father. I longed to see him again. He used to say he would visit me. I waited and waited but he never came. Afterwards, till I was eleven, my grandmother brought me up. She spoiled me. I was fine with her, but then she died too. So I had many losses in childhood. At a certain point I became rebellious: fuck the family! I turned to my friends for company. I figured I wouldn't lose them.

The man who abused me was my best friend Alan's father. I met him a short while after my grandmother died. He quickly became like a father to me. He looked after me, gave me presents ... I used to spend weekends with them. My mother thought it was okay. I made friends quickly. I felt like a member of his family. His son was like a brother to me. This man spoiled me: toys, first of all, then tapes, a radio-cassette player, a small colour television, even a computer. Pocket money too if I didn't have enough.

He was affectionate towards me, but it didn't seem out of the ordinary. In the evening, both of us boys would fall asleep on top of him while we watched movies. He would carry both of us to our beds, just as though he was my father too. In my mind he was treating me just like his own son, so it didn't worry me at all. When he gave me a big present, he also gave one to his son. I didn't see anything wrong in it. But my mother became more and more distrustful. She started worrying and didn't want me to see him any more. She found it suspicious that an adult should be so interested in me. I told myself she had been watching too many bad movies.

On one particular day, he came to fetch me early because I was on holiday from school. His son didn't have a holiday that day. While we were making breakfast, I noticed he was brushing up against me more than usual. But the kitchen was small, so I let it go. Then we went into the living-room and he started to play with me. We were having a friendly wrestling match when I began to realize something else was happening. He had his hand down my shorts. I more or less let him continue – I didn't really know where it would end. Was it real? Was it a joke, or what? I was hesitant, I was surprised, I didn't know what to do. He took off my shorts, then my underwear, and started fondling me. At that point, I realized it was definitely sexual. I got away from him, I ran outside. I hid in the cabana in the garden. He negotiated with me to get me to come out, he told me to forget what had happened, that it wasn't serious, that we should go and fetch Alan. I was afraid to sit next to him in the car. I asked him to drive me home and he did, trying to put things right with me the whole way home.

I refused to see him again after that and I distanced myself from his son too. A little while afterwards, Alan told me his father would have sole custody in future. He invited me again several times, but I never went back.

Before this, that man had been a role model for me. Afterwards I destroyed the mental image I'd had of him. I asked myself: how far would he have gone? How long had he been preparing to move on me? I still ask myself these questions. If I were to see him again, I would let it all out verbally, maybe even physically. I fantasize about hitting him, getting my own back, avenging myself. I've thought about it several times. When I practised boxing or karate, I used to think of him and get super-aggressive. I imagined his face on the punching bag and I pounded him until I was exhausted.

After that experience, I didn't trust any men at all. I lost my ability to trust. Especially with men who look like him. I get along better with women. It's difficult to trust anyone ...
I ought to have suspected something, like my mother had said. I ought to have seen the signs long before ... Sometimes he

would shut himself up in his room telling us not to disturb
him. Maybe he was masturbating while thinking about me ...
Actually, once, for a joke, we walked into his room anyway. He
was on his bed, in his underwear. He was angry with us. We
laughed about it, though. Maybe I was a bit naïve. That man
had no one in his life, never any girlfriends, never any women.
I asked him about it and he told me he didn't want it, that he
was too old, too fat, too ugly. I've always asked myself why
he behaved like that with me. I have some ideas. First of all,
I thought maybe he wanted something in return for all the presents he'd given me. If he was homosexual, perhaps he was
sick of sleeping with old people his own age and wanted to
have someone younger, something like that? But there was
never any indication that he was homosexual. I really don't
know if he was.

If I were to see him today I wouldn't ask him why he did it.
I would demolish him just like he demolished me. He made me
lose my faith in myself and my trust in others. And I walked
right into it: he had the idea in his head for a long time before
it happened, I think. It hurt me so much, he disappointed me
so much ... If I bump into him I'll tell him to get lost, that he's
invading my personal space. If he still bothers me, I'll beat him
up. I don't think it was simply youthful stupidity on his part.
No, that's for sure ...

Before all this happened, homosexuals didn't bother me. It
was none of my business, I couldn't care less; I didn't give a
damn. But now I don't trust homosexuals – I mean men who
are attracted to other men. My mother has very close friends
who are homosexuals. I accept them because I knew them as
people before I knew they were gay. And those particular
homosexuals happen to respect me.

Yesterday I was watching a film, The Crying Game. It's about a
homosexual transvestite. Me, I would have killed him, just like
that. Do you know the story? The main character is looking for
the wife of a man he knew as a prisoner he guarded who
became his friend but has since died. He finds the man's wife
and falls in love with her. It's only when they go to bed that he
discovers he has made a mistake: that there "woman" is a man!
If that happened to me, I'd get so damned mad I'd knock his
head off. Homosexuals should stay away from me. It would be

best for them. The worst was one time when a homo began to
flirt with me. I was walking down the street and this guy
seemed to be following me. I went around the block twice to
make sure he was following me. Then I grabbed him by the
collar and asked him what he was after. He said: "Leave me
alone. I'm not evil, I don't wish you any harm, I just want to
get to know you." I told him straight I didn't want to know
guys like him and I shoved him into the brick wall. That type
disgusts me.

Since I was abused, I often ask myself why he did that to me.
Why didn't he hit on his own son? Why didn't he respect me?
Why didn't he choose some other boy? I've often heard it said
that men who like young boys prefer blonds. It's probably true.
Often, in films where the scene is set in prison, you see the
younger ones being raped by other prisoners. Several will go
after one at the same time. If I ever go to prison, I would prefer
to kill myself rather than live through that. I would say to
them, "You kill me first and then do what you want with my
body." I'm scared to death of being raped. In the Canadian film
Un zoo la nuit there's a scene like that. It was fine with me
when the big fat disgusting pig got demolished.

If the same thing happened to me today, I would defend
myself. I haven't brought charges against him because I just
wanted to write him off, never see him again, even in court.
Because of that affair, I felt rejected all over again. I turned into
a bit of a delinquent. But I'm respectful of people. I wouldn't
rape a girl. I wouldn't abandon my children either. Why do
some people do that? We live in a bizarre world.

It's very infrequent that I walk about undressed, without a
shirt or just in my underwear. Even here, in the group home,
I don't trust anybody. You never know if someone won't masturbate while secretly watching you. At night, when I go to bed,
I go through my whole day in my mind and I ask myself questions. Why did so-and-so do that? What would have happened
if … ? I'm as distrustful as anyone can be, I would say even
paranoid. I'm always afraid someone is looking at me in my
room. The first time I saw a man who looked like the fellow
who abused me, it really set me back. The fellow was supposed to work with me. He was an educator. I didn't want
anything to do with him. He looked just like my abuser.

Today I realize my reaction was exaggerated. But it took me
a long time to realize it.

I have a way of coping that I call "the strongbox." If something upsets me I lock it up inside myself and I don't think
about it any more. That's what I've done with the abuse. It's
only when I meet men who resemble him that I think of that
creep and fear takes over again. As soon as a guy looks at me
I ask myself what he wants.

I was happy to see I could go out with girls. I've only once
spoken with a girl about being abused. She kept it secret and
didn't change how she was with me. In my fantasy world there
is nothing violent. On the contrary, I only see love. I find abuse
disgusting. I'm not the type to want to make others suffer what
was done to me. Sometimes when I see a beautiful girl I say to
myself that if I jumped her I wouldn't hurt her. It's just a way
of speaking: I've never been afraid I'll become a rapist. I'm
more afraid of being raped myself. That's why I'm so distrustful, why I see abusers everywhere.

I'd like a stable relationship with a girl later on. I'm happy
when I have a girl beside me. When you've been abused by a
man and you later find yourself with a girl, it's as if God is
making a dream come true, offering it to you on a silver plat-
ter. It's sad when abused youngsters become homosexual.
That's what I've heard happens. I think such guys were probably already a bit homosexual somehow. I myself like to be with
male friends, but not to have sex with them. To have good
friends, though, is very important. It took me some time before
I had any. You're not homosexual because you have close male
friends, are you?

CHAPTER FOUR

The Secret of the "Men's House": How Victims Perceive Sexual Abuse

When children are sexually abused at a young age, they have no reference point from which to evaluate the meaning of such a traumatising experience. A child or a young adolescent, faced with a situation he can hardly understand, will construct different hypotheses to try and make sense of what is going on, to explain to himself why this is happening to him. He might tell himself, for instance, that his abuser needs affection, or that he has no opportunity to find adult partners. He may see the abuser as wanting to teach him about sexuality; he may think the abuser cannot manage to control his sexual impulses, that he wants a reward for the attention he has given the child. The child may also think that his aggressor has simply misunderstood the relationship between them.

Before looking at the different perceptions of sexual abuse reported by the men who have taken part in this research, we will take a brief detour into anthropology and into history. This will provide a context for some of the social interpretations and cultural justifications surrounding forced sexual activity between men and boys.

Intergenerational sexuality between males is not an unusual phenomenon; far from it. Anthropologist Daniel Welzer-Lang[1] even sees in it one of the rites of passage that constitute the anti-chamber to the Men's House, that is, the symbolic (or real) place of initiation into models of virility. Not only were practices that Westerners now associate with sexual abuse tolerated but they were everyday practice in other countries at other times. One has only to reflect, for example, on the enslavement of many children or, again, on the practices termed "pedagogical" that were prevalent in antiquity, when boys were taken in charge by masculine mentors and sexual relations initiated by the adult were not excluded.

Maurice Godelier tells how the Baruyas of New Guinea force their young ones to fellate their elders. For them "sperm is life, a food which gives strength to life." Secretly, in the Men's House, adolescents are expected to practise fellatio on young unmarried men. Whereas in our society masculine homosexuality is often associated with effeminacy, among the Baruyas homosexual relations are part of learning how to be masculine. Such a practice should, however, remain secret. Those who resist are forced to comply. According to Godelier, "the young initiates, from the time they enter the Men's House, are fed on the sperm of their elders in order to make them grow bigger and stronger than the women, to make them superior to women, capable of dominating and directing them."[2] Forcing the boys to have sexual relations with their elders serves to perpetuate the power structure between the sexes – to maintain the subordination not only of male children but also of women, who are considered to be inferior.

The ethnologist Gilbert Herdt has shown that, among the Sambias of New Guinea, virility is also passed on, from one generation to another, by the sperm produced during sexual relations: "It follows that the men believe that constant ingestion of semen (which they liken to breast feeding) is the only means by which the boys grow, mature and aquire competent manhood. In consequence, beginning with the first stage of initiation, fellatio – to be practised as often as possible – is completely institutionalized ... This behaviour is a huge secret which must not be revealed, on pain of death, to children or to women."[3]

These observations suggest that certain types of intergenerational sexuality tend to reproduce sexual relationships of the dominant-dominated type and the more traditional social-sexual roles: i.e., the young boy must first learn to submit before in turn subjugating those younger than himself, or women. It is to be noted that, in societies that encourage this form of initiation,[4] the sexuality of the boy is in no way considered. Taken to the extreme, the expectation is not that he should derive any pleasure but rather that he should conform to the customs of the culture to which he belongs. The model of non-reciprocal sexuality is therefore transmitted from one generation to the next: the adult male takes what pleases him. The boy who submits against his own wishes can always tell himself that his turn will come. This form of intergenerational and non-reciprocal sexuality thus plays a role even in the transmission of masculine role models: "What has been done to you, you may later do to younger boys, to girls, to women – when you are a man."

Sexual abuse is of course not the only form of initiation into masculinity. Since long ago, physical violence has characterized the passage of males into physiological maturity. A forced initiation into sexuality is a continuation rather than a break with this tradition. For certain men, enslaving other men for their sexual needs is part of the demonstration of their virility. It is even an expression of their power. This is a curious reprise of what has been the predominant reasoning since ancient times, that what was important for a male was that he be sexually active and not passive, whatever the age, sex, and even degree of consent of the targeted partner.[5]

Today's reality is not so very different. Daniel Welzer-Lang stresses that even boys who have not endured aggression or forced sexual initiation by adults know deep down that they might, that the younger and weaker may at any moment be subjected to the will of their elders. Imposed intergenerational sexuality plays a role in the socialization of small boys: when the boy is not actually subjected to the desires of adults, the fear of being so reminds each one that he is an "apprentice" of the masculine condition and that he is obliged to submit to the rules, recognized or secret, of older men. Sexual abuse between males, far from being considered an exception or a blunder on life's way, may from then on be seen as a perpetuation, alas, of a long manly tradition according to which the initiation of the youngest takes place through an apprenticeship in submission, be it sexual or otherwise.[6]

Certain studies suggest that, in our society, sexual interest in children could be far more common than is widely believed. According to an enquiry by J. Briere and M. Runtz, twenty-one percent of their student guinea-pigs experienced some erotic attraction towards children, nine percent had sexual fantasies involving children, five percent masturbated during these fantasies, and seven percent were disposed to having sexual relations with children if they were assured of not being discovered or punished.[7] Abuse fantasies are not, then, particularly a marginal phenomenon. It is possible that men, who have been culturally encouraged to imagine their partners, whatever their sex, to be smaller and more slender, will have a tendency to project this eroticism on to those who are appreciably younger, and even towards those who are not yet pubescent.

Canons of beauty often valorize "pedomorphic" qualities, i.e., those appropriate to youth only. It is striking how often advertisements, for example, remove adult characteristics such as body hair or aging skin, on masculine models as much as on feminine ones. Whatever their real age, erotic fantasy bodies must look young, indeed juvenile and vulnerable. Since masculine socialization has traditionally insisted that man must be in the dominant position, sexual abuse could be situated somewhere along this line of "logic": the abused seems conceived as a submissive young partner.

The historic and cultural explanations for intergenerational sexual relations and sexual abuse form a background to each victim's rationalizations. The perception of the boy victim varies according to the motivation he accords his aggressor, be it retribution, misunderstanding, imposition of power, or a wish to tarnish the child or initiate him into the ways of sex. The real point of view of the aggressor is absent from this research except, of course, when the victim has himself become an aggressor – which happens in some instances.

The way an individual perceives the world affects his way of adapting to it. Hence it is useful to examine how the abused boy interprets the behaviour of his aggressor. His perception of the abuse he endures and his resulting perception of masculine sexuality will explain why the abused young person has kept silent, why he has not asked for help, or why he has not believed anyone could help him. His view of things will also show why, afterwards, he has turned his anger against others, notably through delinquent acts or by sexually abusing younger children; or, again, why he has resorted to such self-destructive behaviour as drug abuse, self-mutilation, or attempted suicide. Five relatively different perceptions stand out in the testimonies. Sometimes the perceptions overlap.

Unbridled Sexuality

"He was unable to control himself," many boys will spontaneously say of their aggressor. The myth that sexuality can be stronger than everything, stronger than self, is certainly not new. It has all too often served to rationalize, indeed to legitimize, abuse of all sorts, and not only from the point of view of the aggressors, which would be understandable, but also from the point of view of the victims, which seems, at first sight, more astonishing.

The belief in an uncontrollable compulsion arises from an essentialist and naturalistic conception of sexuality. The sexual revolution has spread this notion throughout western culture; sexuality is the result of an irrepressible impulse.[8] By virtue of this myth, men are without resistance when it comes to certain impulses arising in the depths of their being – be it from their genes, their hormones, their neurons, or their libido – take your choice. When sexuality is conceived and presented as a need as vital as the need to nourish oneself, for example, restraining it is hardly imagineable. Abusers take pains to have their victims accept such reasoning.

It is then understandable that a boy or a young man can be tempted to explain and, up to a point, excuse in this way the aggressions he has suffered: his aggressor cannot control himself or has not managed to overcome his basic impulses. This is the point of view, for example, of Charles, incest victim at fourteen years of age. Charles suspects that his father was molested and that he internalized the dynamic of abuse, which would explain why he has repeated the abuse with his own sons. It is also the case with Matthew, sexually aggressed by the father of his best friend. Matthew, as we have seen, believes that his abuser, who was not very attractive, divorced, and lonely, had hardly any other possibility of obtaining sexual gratification. He often complained that he was too fat and was not the type to please women. Matthew was there, to hand, so to speak. Francis, an incest victim, also believed his father, who told him he was obliged to have sexual relations with his son because his wife refused to satisfy him. Jean-Marc, aggressed by a cousin, asks himself whether the cousin was not, at such moments, in the grip of some kind of madness: "Is he crazy? Sometimes I didn't know what to think any more: he would be quiet, sweet, buy me chocolate. Other times, when I didn't want to, he became violent. Once, he took out a knife so I wouldn't resist. Then I knew he was going too far and I spoke to my mother about it." As this last case demonstrates, it is necessary at times for the aggressor to go very far in the eyes of his victim before the victim stops considering the abuse as something that derives from primitive but normal human sexual behaviour.

A Sexual Initiation

Sexual abuse is often seen as sexual initiation by the abused child or adolescent because the aggressor presents it as such. Like the initiation model described by historians and anthropologists, forced sexual relations between males of different generations can still be considered to be part of a secret rite. Thus, Francis' father explicitly gave his son to understand that their sexual play would help Francis learn about sex until he was able to have relations with girls. The falsity of the explanation didn't occur to the adolescent until he began to go out with girls: his father then became extremely jealous. Andrew's father also presented the sexual relations to which he subjected his son as a form of sexual initiation, telling him that he would show him what adult genitals looked like, teach him a good way to masturbate, and instruct him in the art of massage, etc. The boy was caught up in a spiral in which he could no longer distinguish the difference between legitimate sexual information and abuse.

In cases of sexual abuse, the aggressors rarely see themselves as aggressors; this makes it easier to persuade the victims that they are being initiated, not abused. Without an aggressor, after all, can aggression exist? In most of the cases we came across, the "initiator," even when faced with legal proceedings, continued to deny or minimize his responsibility. Moreover, most aggressors have a tendency to define themselves as exclusively heterosexual and declare themselves to be homophobic into the bargain[9]: they see themselves as "real men" endowed with the right to sexually initiate others. This would tend to confirm that, in general, it is not the homosexual nature of the act that arouses abusers, since they are not generally of that orientation, but the power relationship that surrounds the sexual abuse.

Some contemporary authors,[10] mindful of ancient rituals of initiation, emphasize the so-called pedagogical aspect of sexual relations between children and adults. But if a degree of paedophilia was indeed considered as initiatory in the past, the practice was still abusive. The willingness of the young person was not considered at the time, and many of these young people were slaves. This said, during antiquity sexual aggression committed against free citizens was condemned and most laws recognized the existence of rape, including that of boys by adult men, and punished it.[11] Thus, the idea that our concept of sexual aggression was unknown in an idealized antiquity is erroneous. What's more, boys who were violated at the time reacted much as their counterparts do today. Suetonius the historian, for example, wrote about the shame of two young boys who had been raped by the emperor Tiberius, who, on learning "that they both blamed each other for their disgrace,"[12] had their legs broken. It is therefore aberrant, in the context of abuse to point to those civilizations where children were quite happily treated as slaves or sexual objects. Nor must consensual homosexual relations and sexual abuse be confounded: my definition of abuse as given earlier eliminates all such confusion.

To come back to the men involved in this enquiry, it is important to note that the more a young boy feels sexually stimulated or later experiments with homosexual attractions or acts, the more he accepts the view that what was going on originally was a form of sexual initiation. But it may be wholly inaccurate to conclude that his main sexual orientation will be homosexual.

Many people, including victims of abuse, believe falsely that an erection or, more significantly, ejaculation signifies pleasure and implies voluntary participation. This is not so. Sustained physiological stimulation or, again, simply the fact of being nude is liable to engender a state of excitement, not to mention the fact that fear, anxiety, or the feeling of doing something forbidden can have quite paradoxical effects. The brain and the body can sometimes register opposed impressions, which can lead to dissonance on the cognitive level. The psychological and physical reactions of an individual are not always in agreement with one another. That a boy should have an erection is too easily interpreted as a sign of consent or of enjoyment; what is forgotten is that a mechanical physical reaction can occur even in cases of rape.

That homosexual or bisexual tendencies appear in the adolescent or the young man who has been sexually abused also reinforces the myth of initiation. Such a situation is wrongly translated as proof that the young person was able to "seduce" his aggressor. His relative passivity, already deemed suspicious under the presumption that a man always knows how to defend himself (even if he is five years old), is falsely taken as informed consent. In reality, is stems more from obedience ("It was my father, I had to obey him") or from curiosity ("I really didn't know what he was going to do. I wanted to see what was going to happen"); or it is attributed to the fact that the young person was taken by surprise ("It was the first time it happened to me. I didn't know how to react"). In no way does any subsequent manifestation of homosexuality signify that a boy wanted to be aggressed. Those men we questioned who are today of homosexual or bisexual orientation do not seem to suffer any less from the aftereffects of the aggressions they suffered. Far from it. To see in his homosexual orientation a sign that a boy wanted to be abused or enjoyed being abused is a ludicrous notion. No one would entertain the idea that the ultimate heterosexuality of a female victim of sexual abuse could lessen the crime of which she was the target. Even when the sexual abuse provided a measure of physical or psychological gratification, not one boy spoke of it in terms of pleasure. It is generally very difficult to know, moreover, whether the homosexual or bisexual orientation of an abuse victim developed before or after his ordeal, since most of the abuse took place when the victim was very young.

To sum up, when the perpetrator of abuse portrays his acts as an altruistic "sexual education," and when the young person gets a certain gratification, the event is all the more likely to be seen as sexual initiation rather than abuse. This perception protects the aggressor from denunciation, at least to begin with, since the boy sees himself as having complied with his initiator. This perception, if it does not change, may in the long term falsify the young man's vision of sexuality (or, should it be the case, homosexuality). Perception of abuse as a form of initiation is likely to encourage the victim to paint his abuse in erotic colours. It may also encourage him to behave in a similar fashion.

A Situation of Domination

According to Daniel Welzer-Lang, in learning what it means to be a man, there seem to be no grey areas. One is either active or passive, aggressed against or an aggressor. This is how a young man learns the relationship based on permanent force. Whoever forgets this rule becomes a designated victim. Any deviation from the rule for emotional reasons is seen as something left over from childhood, the reappearance in a male of something from the world of females. All sentimentality must therefore be fought against, indeed punished: "If you want to be like a woman you will be treated like a woman."[13]

Certain young people learn quickly to integrate a parallel logic: this masculine dictum, pronounced by those who are the strongest and the biggest, quickly appears in their own sexuality. In this they follow in the footsteps of their aggressors. Paul, used as a sexual object by his father, then by his brothers and by one of his sisters, has indeed been led to perceive sexual arousal as a synonym for taking over and dominating. It is significant that, while still an adolescent, he himself began to sexually abuse the young children of his older brothers. Once a correlation has been established between submission and sexual pleasure, it can appear quite normal to impose, or to imagine oneself imposing, all sorts of sexual activities. The unwritten law of masculine domination, of which Daniel Welzer-Lang writes, reinforces this perception: the weakest, smallest, and most vulnerable have no choice but to accept their fate as whipping-boys. Does this not constitute part of learning what "real" masculinity is all about?

Looking not only at the sexual dimension of sexual abuse but also at the power relationship it expresses makes all the more sense when a majority of men who abuse boys describe themselves as heterosexual. It is not so much the need to express a homosexual impulse that arouses their appetite so much as a need to impose their power and their will on the victim. Numerous child abusers are attracted indiscriminately by girls and boys alike. Some respondents told us that their brothers and sisters were also abused by the man who abused them. It is possible, however, that certain aggressors much prefer to abuse young males since dominating a male is symbolically more gratifying, therefore more exciting, from their point of view, than dominating a female.

In every era, conquering warriors have flaunted their domination over the enemy's soldiers by raping their women and children – and sometimes raping the enemies themselves.[14] So obviously sexuality does not necessarily have to do with pleasure. It can conceal negative, destructive, even murderous meanings. The imposition of sexual relations obeys the same dynamic as the imposition of force or the imposition of ideas. It is a tyrannical act, a denial of liberty, a denial of the other's integrity at its most intimate bodily level. Those who have lived through a parallel situation over a prolonged period of time feel dispossessed of their selfhood. One respondent stated that, in some small way, he felt very close to understanding the desperation of concentration camp victims. Boys who have lived through the enslavement of abuse are among those most inclined to self-mutilation or suicidal ideation: this body, used as an object by the aggressor, is superfluous and can be discarded. Activities involving painful penetration of the body (whether anal rape or insertion of an adult penis into the throat of a child until he chokes or vomits) or a degradation of the child (beating the boy, urinating or defecating on him) count among the most damaging; his personal integrity is denied and altered. Acts that would be extremely difficult for an adult to make sense of are imposed on children who are incapable of seeing anything rational in the situation at all, and might conclude from it that the world is crazy, and if not the world, then they themselves.

Planned Revenge

The concept of revenge was brought up most frequently by abused boys who had in turn committed sexual abuse. If they wanted thereby to avenge or exorcise the abuse they lived through, why should it not be the same for their aggressor? Such logic brings some respondents to conceive of their own abuse as a revenge that was more or less planned by their aggressor. It is often underestimated how vengeful violence, whatever its manifestations, can be adopted as a way of life by certain males. For such men, it would work in the same way as a drug. Psychologist Rollo May[15] has written that to make others suffer is one way to prove that one exists. In making an impression on others, a torturer sees himself as all powerful. To make another male suffer would be one of the ultimate proofs of a virile superiority. The violence is always odious, but it is part of our humanity: a forced relationship obliging another to recognize one's needs and to satisfy one's desires.

Abusers' victims learn it very fast: a situation of sexual abuse is one in which the sexual scenarios are decided unilaterally. The aggressor imposes his desires, whereas in an egalitarian relationship, he must negotiate them with his male or female partner. In sexually abusive situations, once the resistance of the child or adolescent has been overcome, the elder can impose his most secret, most shameful, even his most degrading propensities.

Some of the scenes described by the men in this study were of unimaginable brutality: being torn during anal penetration, being obliged to practise fellatio despite repeated vomiting, being severely beaten, being sprayed with urine or covered with excrement. It is difficult not to see in such acts a manifestation of hatred. To young people who have been thus abused – tortured sexually, physically, and psychologically – the sadistic motivation of the aggressor is clear.

In some cases, events unfolded as if the aggressors were seeking consciously to degrade or vilify the child or adolescent in order to carry out some vengeance upon him. In some cases, the youth would indeed learn that his torturer had himself been a victim of sexual cruelty at a young age. Being forced to discover sexuality in all its most sordid aspects is not without consequence. Out of this will sometimes result a "traumatized" sexuality in which the ex-victim will not cease to try and exorcise his sorry state of existence. In this manner, Paul, aggressed, humiliated and degraded by his brothers, develops an extremely negative image of himself: in his own eyes he is nothing but a trashcan. Hardly socialized, he has already turned towards young children to satisfy himself sexually. Francis, obliged to sodomize his father, was incapable of giving any meaning whatever to his experience. That same evening, he had done his worst bad trip on drugs. Andrew, sodomized savagely by his father, remained badly traumatized by the experience. His first sexual relationship with a boy – whom he loved – ended abruptly when he tried to imitate his father's conduct.

A certain number of men, having been enslaved by their elders, will themselves know the call of vengeance. Why be surprised, then, that sexual violence perpetuates itself from one generation to another? "Make a man of yourself" – doesn't that mean, "Learn to withstand the violence of your peers and of your elders so you can transmit it later to those younger than yourself"? Exclusively masculine environments, such as the army, or prison, provide a sad example of this: the dominated one aspires eventually to assume the role of dominator. His survival depends on it. A young person is all the more likely to want to abuse others if he himself has been a victim of violence and become less than a man in his own eyes. One of the most eloquent ways to regain his virility, on a symbolic level, is to subjugate someone more vulnerable than himself. This is why vengeance is only rarely directed against the original perpetrator of the initial aggression.

I do not suggest, obviously, that all those men to whom violence has been done will spontaneously become violent. This is not the case. But they all want to know at least why such things have happened. In order to find out, a certain number of ex-victims will risk venturing into enemy territory; some among them will get a taste for it. When a man's very first sexual relations are associated with strong feelings of despair and bitterness, is it surprising that his eroticism should be directed towards vengeance? It is at least a possibility, especially when there have been few other mitigating experiences. That his torturer was evidently untouched by his victim's disinclination or distress leads the victim to see the abuse as a form of ritualized violence from which no one escapes.

A Misunderstanding

Some young men see their abuse quite simply as the result of a tragic misunderstanding. Two different points of view emerge here. The first is that the adult must have mistaken for sexual attraction something akin to a search for affection on the part of the child. Those who have been assaulted by older brothers or by third parties with whom they were already acquainted are the most likely to express this view of things. Pierre, a lonely child who felt rejected by his family, explains that his looking for physical closeness and attention was probably wrongly interpreted by his older brother. The same thing comes out in Joseph's case: the young one goes along with what is being done to him because he thinks that he may at last be loved and accepted by his older brother. Marcel, who was abused by a neighbour, shares this view: he kept visiting the man because in his view he had finally found someone to care for him.

The second source of misunderstanding, which relates most often to extrafamilial abuse, rests on the assumption that the aggressor, who feels he has devoted a great deal of time and money to the boy, would like in one way or another to be repaid, and repaid "in kind." This misunderstanding arises particularly when the boy really has the impression that he is in the aggressor's debt and that it is something he can repay only with his own body. What else could he offer that would please the adult? Matthew's story fits this picture exactly: dreadfully spoiled by the father of his best friend, he feels at once betrayed and ashamed of being naïve when the adult in question gets close to him and then proceeds to have sex with him. James, taken in around the age of thirteen when he was a runaway, follows the same reasoning: how can he disappoint his benefactor?

The perception of abuse as misunderstanding also makes it plain that numerous men have a tendency to sexualize the affection they give or receive. As we have seen, the testimonies of boy victims of incest are eloquent in this regard: almost all of them insisted that the only times their fathers paid them any attention or showed them any affection or tenderness was before, during, or just after sexual relations. When the adult is incapable of seeing the difference between abuse, affection, and sexuality, one can imagine that the child or adolescent he is abusing will be even less capable of distinguishing between the two; hence his confusion, sense of guilt, and above all the feeling that perhaps he is the one who does not know what is going on.

OLIVER'S STORY

Oliver was abused from the age of five by his young uncle and again at twelve by his mother's lover. Oliver is now thirty-nine years old.

The main thing about my childhood, apart from the sexual abuse, was that I didn't see much of my father. It affected me a lot. My father worked eighty hours a week. When he got home, he needed to relax. He found us kids hard to take so it was tough on us when he came home. Sometimes he was violent. By the time I was four, I had welts on my body where he thrashed me with a belt. Apart from that, as far as I remember, I had a normal childhood.

When my mother went out, my father's brother babysat. He was a teenager. His parents, my grandparents, lived nearby. He was about twelve I think, and I was five. He began asking me to perform oral sex on him. I really didn't understand what he wanted but I was afraid to say no. Of course I thought it was odd. I knew it wasn't the sort of thing that happened every day. It makes a huge impression on a kid. It made such a mark on me that to this day I can still go over all the details in my mind as though it was yesterday. I had no idea how to go about it: he showed me how.

I didn't like it. It was as though the clock stopped and time stood still around me, as if I was losing consciousness ... I never told anyone about it. He called it "making love." But I didn't see anything loving about it. It happened several times. I can't say how many because what I remember most vividly are the very first times. It stopped when I got bigger. I was older. So was he.

Later, it was my mother's lover who abused me. I was about twelve or thirteen. In other words, when my uncle stopped abusing me, my mother's lover took over. He was a good friend of my father and stayed at the house some evenings after they played cards. When my father wasn't there, he slept with my mother. Otherwise, he slept in my room, in my bed with me. I had my own room at the time. One morning, as I was waking up, I noticed he was masturbating me. When something like that happens to you, you ask yourself questions. My first reaction was surprise. I moved away from him. I felt uneasy but I had the impression he had gone back to sleep. Anyway, that's what I thought at the time: perhaps he did it in his sleep, without being aware. I didn't know how to react except by trying to squeeze away from him. He turned over on his other side. Maybe what he was doing was what he was dreaming. It happened a dozen or so times, always the same way.

Today, thinking about it, I'm carrying a lot of baggage. I don't like to talk about it. I didn't question it when it happened. I just let him do it, and I tried not to think about what was going on. But I would have liked to know if other kids were going through the same thing. I didn't ask because I was afraid of what the answers would be. It stopped when he no longer came to the house. Maybe it didn't work any more with my mother. Maybe my father became suspicious about him and my mother.

About the same time, when I was twelve or thirteen, I found my mother and him making love together. The bedroom door wasn't properly closed. It upset me to see them because my mother was still living with my father and I couldn't accept that she would cheat on him. But she knew we wouldn't say anything about it because my father would react very badly. He could kill. But the sight of my mother having oral sex with a stranger had aroused me. Looking at them, I was aware of being sexually excited. I went back to my room. It was the first time I masturbated.

As a teenager, I seemed to be different from the other guys: because I was a victim of sexual abuse; because I had seen my mother making love with a stranger; because I too became an abuser. I abused my sisters. It all began with caressing. We knew it was wrong, but we did it just the same because we were brought up in that kind of atmosphere. All the same, my sisters were more or less consenting. We all lacked affection, we were all on the same wavelength. Really, it was sexual play. No penetration. My sisters were younger than I was. It went on until I was fifteen or sixteen. They got interested in boyfriends and they both left home quite young.

It was later on that I committed a real abuse. Five years ago I abused a little girl of seven. I was on drugs. I'm not a paedophile. It was the drink, the drugs, the whole context. I had been

drinking, and I'd done coke. She was my live-in girlfriend's
little daughter. I used to like to stroke her but one evening
I overstepped the limits. I went into her room, took down her
panties, and fondled her with one hand while masturbing
myself with the other. She slept on. Later, I ended up confess-
ing to her mother. She forgave me. But her daughter didn't
forgive me.

In the beginning, I had been afraid to tell my girlfriend. But
then I did tell her the truth, that I'd been behaving like that
since I was a young guy. She herself had already been raped by
her father. That's why she forgave me for what I did. She thinks
I could learn to control myself if I go for therapy. I'm beginning therapy right now. It was the first time I spoke openly
about my problem. It may take me years to come out of it,
I know. But I have to start somewhere.

The first time I had sex with a woman, I didn't really like it
right away. It was winter and it was cold. Across the street from
my house a woman was waiting for a tow-truck for her car. Her
lover, a friend of mine, had gone to the garage. I asked her to
come in. She was pretty fat. I talked her up a bit, flirted with
her. She came back later. She was the first woman I had intercourse with. It's as though I have a fixation about her. Since
then, I've been attracted to big women. With her I had discovered something new. But my sex life has remained kind of passive. I like to go to bed with a girl but generally it's the girl
who makes the first move. I don't like to run after anyone.
I'm not a sex maniac; I don't take much initiative in that way.
That's okay with me. After what I have gone through, I could
have become a sex maniac.

I like to masturbate. Like to play the exhibitionist, too. I've
done that since I was a teenager. I've even been arrested by the
police for it. It always happens in a special context. When I'm
drunk, on drugs, something inside me wakes up. I stand outside a house, in the garden, in front of people's windows and
show myself off. Then I masturbate, sometimes even ejaculate
in front of them. It's always women, just women. In the beginning I used to leave the windows and curtains open at home
and parade about in the nude. I liked the turn-on. Then I went
out to do it. I found that even more exciting. I was caught three

times. I was fined and got six months probation each time. The last time was quite recently.

When I do the exhibitionism thing, I think of the abuse I went through. I think again about my mother and I imagine her completely nude having sex with my father's best friend ... Maybe it's like I'm getting revenge. If the woman joins in my game, I get even more excited. A woman who is disgusted, who's frightened, that excites me less. It's surprising but there are women who play the game. Quite honestly, the very first time I did that, right away I liked it. But the next day, I found it disgusting; I couldn't find enough bad things to say about myself.

What I like to fantasize about mainly are the partners I've already had. In spite of what I've done, I don't have fantasies about children. I won't deny that I like young girls, say from about fifteen years old up to about twenty. That's perfectly normal and it doesn't prevent me from appreciating older women. On the contrary. Yes, I'm attracted to adolescents. When they run after you, what are you going to do? I had a girlfriend who was fourteen years old when I was twenty-six. She looked older. Never mind if it was illegal. I know it was. But she wanted it.

Nothing out of the ordinary was going on the day I first abused my live-in girlfriend's little girl. I just felt it was something I wanted to try. I didn't do it very often. In the end I denounced myself. The little one lives with her grandmother today. She had called Youth Protection and denounced me at the same time I was looking for help myself. I didn't deny it. She too is in therapy. It has left its mark on her although I think the folks in her family made too much of it by totally blackening my character. They said I was evil, that I deserved to go to prison and all ... But she was asleep when I did it. How could I have traumatized her?

I've always kept my secret to myself, regarding the abuse I went through and what I did myself. Today, it's all coming out. I kept it locked up inside me for too long. Why is it I repeated such behaviour afterwards? Why? It's a question I ask myself. I don't know the answer. And even though I saw my uncle rape my sister, I didn't say anything because he had given me some money and asked me to keep quiet. I kept quiet. Why?

Those of us who have been abused run more risk of being scarred by it or of becoming abusers themselves I think. When I did it, maybe I wanted to get my own back. I'm sorry I saw my mother making love with her boyfriend. I would have liked to sleep with her just to punish her, to get my revenge. I told her later on that I saw it all. I have it in for her, bear a grudge against her, because it's her fault I became the way I am. She taught me about sex without self-respect, without any respect for others. I've got it in for women in general because of that. To me they're all sluts, like my mother. When I make love, you know, I'm a very gentle fellow. With certain women some vengeance will surface, but not with all. Most of the women I've made love with were not aware of what was going on inside me.

Andrew, twenty-three years old, was a victim of incest between the ages of thirteen and sixteen.

My name is Andrew. I'm thirty-three and I live outside Quebec. That is why, in response to Michel Dorais' ad about his research on male victims of sexual abuse in childhood, I'm sending my testimony in writing and on cassette.

Until I was seventeen, I lived in a small town. I was thirteen the first time my father abused me. He was then about forty or forty-two years old. My sexual relations with him went on for at least three years after that first abuse. It then took me several years to recover.

I had an ordinary childhood. I am the second of five children in a modest working-class family, originally from Britain. I remember we used to go camping and horse riding during the holidays. Then, I used to have friends and I was a child just like the others, like my brothers and sisters. But when I became a teenager, and even a little before that, I became aware of my sexuality and soon realized I was attracted to other males. I became withdrawn, and I isolated myself. It was during this period that I was abused.

My parents' marriage was breaking up and, that particular evening, I remember, my mother had gone out. My father came home and, for one reason or another, we found ourselves in his car, talking together. I forget what we were talking about but at a certain point the subject of sex came up. My father said to me: "Come on, I'll show you something." He started the car and we drove out of town.

We drove off the highway and turned on to a narrow roadway. I remember tall trees on either side of the car. He said he had to get out to pee and I joined him. Maybe I glanced at his penis – out of curiosity as much as anything. When we got back in the car, he asked me if I had seen a grown man's penis before. I told him no. He took out his penis and showed it me. Then he asked to see mine. I showed it. He wanted to know if I masturbated and offered to show me how to do it "properly." He took my penis in his hand and masturbated me until I got a hard-on and urged me to do the same thing to him. Afterwards, he took my penis in his mouth. I immediately came close to ejaculation. I didn't know people could do that. My father asked me to suck on his penis, in order, he said, to show me how it should be done. Then we took off our pants. He asked me to turn on my side, to bend over on the seat, facing the back of the car. That's when he raped me. He sodomized me. I remember crying out when he penetrated me. I thought I was going to die. But in spite of everything, I had been aroused, something I was discovering for the first time. However, the pain blocked everything else out. When he reached orgasm inside me, I was crying. When he had finished, he wiped off the car and tried to calm me. We went back to the house. I don't remember how it all ended. Maybe he went to bed, I don't know.

I've never told anyone what happened. My father was never punished. I didn't know anyone who had been sexually abused and there was no one I could talk to about it. I kept my feelings to myself. I felt betrayed, isolated, incapable of loving, incapable of being loved.

About six months later, my father left home and went to live with my grandmother. We went there for weekends. One evening, when I was getting ready for bed, my father asked me to give him a massage. His work was physically very hard and he often had a sore back, so I said yes. He undressed completely. Myself, I was just in my underpants and when he turned on his back he asked me to take them off. That night, we began a codependent sexual relationship. Whenever he asked me for a massage, it was a signal for sexual relations. It was mutual masturbation or mutual fellatio. He never tried to sodomize me again. Often, when the sex was over, we used to talk about school, about my mother, about all sorts of things. It was more or less the only time we talked to each other.

As a teenager, I remember feeling isolated, depressed. I hoped the day would come when I would no longer feel anything. The only relationships I had with boys of my own age were sexual and superficial. I couldn't keep any friends. I felt vulnerable and scared. I had problems at school. School bored me. I left school. I was placed in a private school to finish my year. There I met Mark who was to become my closest friend for a period of two years. We were inseparable, we did everything together. The last time we saw each other, we had spent the whole afternoon at the beach. That evening, we went to his father's summer cottage. We were all alone there. Mark and I drank a few bottles of beer and smoked some hash he had brought. When we went to bed, I initiated some sexual activity. I was attracted to him and I was wondering what it would be like to have sex with him. My hand slipped over his body and I slowly removed his underwear. I gave him oral sex and he did the same for me. Afterwards I turned him over and entered him, maybe more brutally than he would have wished. He wanted to do the same with me, but I refused.

When we returned home, I never heard from him again. At school, other teenagers hassled me and threatened me, saying they knew I was a fag. I left school for good then. Some months later I went to live with one of my aunts, very far from where I was born. I took up my studies there.

When I grew up, I began living on my own. Again I moved to another town. At first I never went out at all. Then friends from work took me to a local gay bar and I started going there on my own. I also went to social gatherings where I met people. I slept with many men. The only thing I never did was anal sex.

In spite of everything, I was afraid of intimacy, of friendship. I still find it difficult to trust anyone and I find it hard to believe others could find me attractive. I've remained quite solitary over the years. I had to wait a long time to find a man who would make love to me gently; he was the only one I agreed to have anal sex with. Since then I've had other relationships, some based on sex and others based on friendship.

In my sexual fantasies I like to be the dominant one, but from time to time I have fantasies where I'm someone's slave and I'm forced to obey him. I've tried this out in real life two or three times but I discovered it doesn't really appeal to me. The most satisfying relationship I've had was in a partnership where each of us could alternate between a passive and active or aggressive role, as the mood took us. Whether it be in fantasy or in reality, my partners are the same age as myself and like me in body weight.

I have chosen to forget and put away in a little box in my head everything that happened to me during my adolescence. It has cost me dearly because I missed out on my childhood. I am

reminded of it when I speak to others, and above all by the
way I get into a relationship, which contrasts with the way
other people approach relationships. Today, at this point in my
life, I accept that I'm gay; I'm even happy about it. I am still
somewhat reserved and ill at ease. But I'm more trusting now,
I can express my feelings and I have less fear of being rejected
or of becoming emotionally dependent on someone. I go out
from time to time and I have sexual relationships that are satisfying most of the time. I'm becoming more and more at ease
with my chosen lifestyle.

CHAPTER FIVE

Coming to Terms with Abuse: Confused Emotions

The boy who has been abused carries a significant psychological wound that is not only difficult to heal but often worsens over time. The more the wound is denied, hidden, or neglected, the more it makes itself felt in different physical, psychological, and relational symptoms. As one respondent said, "It's like a time bomb inside you," an invisible weapon that cannot be prevented from exploding because no one understands its mechanism well enough.

It is difficult to establish a posteriori the cause-and-effect linkages between the trauma of sexual abuse and the problems experienced later by young male victims, since many young men present analogous psychological and relational problems without ever having been abused. In order to prove the existence of causal links between sexual abuse and subsequent problems experienced by ex-victims, it would be necessary to compare, over time, the evolution of boys from similar backgrounds who were abused with those who were not. But if or ethical and practical reasons this is impossible.

This does not mean, however, that no attempt should be made to understand the after-effects of sexual abuse by looking at what has become of those who have gone through it. The repetitive nature of the ongoing difficulties experienced by the thirty young men questioned within the framework of this enquiry cannot but demand our attention. Is it not reasonable to hypothesize that the problems they have in common are due to the sexual abuse they experienced?

Sexual abuse often brings confusion, if not cognitive dissonance, in its wake, hence the title given to this chapter.[1] Cognitive confusion arises when the boy no longer knows what to think or how to interpret what is happening to him. Cognitive dissonance arises when a discordance, an inconsistency or a split shows up when he attempts cognitively to assimilate contradictory information. In both cases, the process of constructing reality is clouded. The individual comes to experience disparate or paradoxical emotions. In reviewing precise contexts in which the sexual abuse of boys has occurred, we have found parallel situations taking many different faces.

Affection or Exploitation?

"I didn't know what to think," many respondents have declared. Between the time when the attention he is getting seems to be something positive in the boy's existence (before the abuser has revealed his ultimate intentions) and the moment when the sexual abuse begins or is repeated, there is a sharp dividing line. The youngster is bound to be confused about a person who has become significant to him but who is also abusing him. "Does he really love me? Is it because he is weak or sick that he does such things? Is he sorry about it? Could I, without wanting to, have caused these things to happen? What if it was just a mistake and won't happen again?"

In many cases, an initial relationship of trust is only gradually transformed into a feeling of betrayal or exploitation. This gradual deterioration will bring about some bewilderment in the mind of the child concerning his own guilt or responsibility. All children love to get attention. Perpetrators know this and play on the ambiguity of their relationship with the child. Most children internalize an attitude of obedience towards adults. Even when adults ask of them things that seem incomprehensible, children will assume it is "for their own good." As the testimonies in this book demonstrate, even once a child has realized that a relationship is abusive and that he is hurt by it, he will look for reasons to explain why his abuser has behaved as he has. He will tend to minimize the seriousness of the situation and tell himself that by tolerating it he is at least receiving some attention. He may also try to convince himself that the abusive act will not recur. Since his abuser never suggests that the relationship is abnormal but treats it as a secret game, a mutual exchange of services, an initiation, or a normal gesture of affection, the child comes to doubt his own judgment. Is he right to resist? Is he the object of love or legitimate desires, even if this type of love and desire seems burdensome to him? Since the boys most vulnerable to sexual abuse are those most in need of tenderness and attention from an adult, they are all the more willing to tolerate the abuse. After all, they are experiencing one of those rare moments when an adult is taking notice of them: the child who has never been caressed is happy at last to be fondled; the child who is rejected is proud at last to be acknowledged. Thus, these children will allow themselves to be imprisoned gradually by the man who can rescue them from a state in which they are deprived of affection or parental attention.

Many boys come to believe that a sexual relationship between youths and adults is common, even though clandestine. Some will believe that, by accepting such intimacies, they make their fathers or brothers happier and thus more likely to show understanding towards them. They perceive sexual contact as an opportunity to receive the kind of attention they would otherwise be refused. Others fear that, should they refuse, they will lose the friendship of the adult who says he loves them. This confusion is often accentuated by the fact that these boys hardly communicate with those close to them. As a result there are very few adults to whom they can turn if they wish to question what they are experiencing.

Once he has been subjected to abuse, and especially if it has happened more than once, the young boy is surprised to find that the affection he craves is not reciprocated. The expectations of the protagonists are badly matched. The one seeks attention and protection; the other is looking for sexual gratification. Many young boys, caught off guard, blame themselves for the "misunderstanding." Perhaps their behaviour led the aggressor to believe they wanted to get sexually involved with him. Maybe sexual favours are the price they have to pay if they want attention from those older than themselves. As soon as the aggressor's affection, his gifts, or even the diffidence he inspires no longer seem so important to the youngster, he understands that he has mistaken the abuser's taking advantage of him for affection.

Stranger in His Own Body

When it continues, sexual abuse puts a boy in a situation where he feels cut off from his own body and from his sexuality. Something inside him has been stolen. Worse, if he is unable to extricate himself from the aggressor's hold over him, he will cut himself off little by little from his own feelings; he will arm himself against that from which there is no escape; he will, in short, become a stranger in his own body.

To protect himself against the repeated invasion of his deepest inner self, the abused boy may in some way turn off the connection between his mind and his body. Several have confirmed that, when younger, they acquired the ability to "leave their body." While being abused, they could escape from it. It was as though the abuse was not happening to them but just to their bodies. This schizophrenic separation, this split, this flight from or denial of reality is one of several defence or survival mechanisms reported by the respondents.

In a similar vein, many of the boys have developed a sexuality that is based almost entirely on the giving of pleasure to their partner and the putting aside of their own sexual needs. In so doing, it is as though they have permanently integrated the derogation of their own person to the rank of sexual object and thus abdicated their own right to sexual pleasure. It is not suprising that many of these boys later prostitute themselves more or less mechanically or stay with partners they have not really chosen to be with. They see sexual relations as a necessary evil, at worst a difficult moment to get through, at best a duty.

Several ex-victims are deprived of all sexual pleasure because of the memories that flood in on them during sexual encounters. Some say they have managed only very slowly to overcome the problem. "The first time I felt anything at all, it was twelve years later! Even with girls I loved, I hardly felt anything when they touched me." Or: "It took me a long time to realize that I too had sexual needs over and above just going through the motions to bring my wife to orgasm." Many of the respondents have been left with a fear of being touched, a fear of being abused again. "It burns like fire when someone touches me, or I freeze up, or I strike out. I don't want anyone to get too close to me."

The body awareness of young men who have earlier been victims of sexual abuse is sometimes even more problematic. With them, self-mutilation can be interpreted not only as an attempt to dissociate from their body but also as a form of self-punishment. The body is being reprimanded for having felt something; perhaps it is being made less attractive. Self-infliction of physical pain may also serve as a distraction from emotional pain. Paradoxically, self-destruction may also represent to the young man proof that he is reclaiming responsibility for the body that he did not previously regard as his own.

Efforts to rid oneself of memories and of a body that are sources of pain may lead to suicidal thoughts or suicidal attempts. Recent research shows the gravity of the problem.[2] More than a third of the men I interviewed reported that they had seriously considered suicide. Several had made at least one attempt. Trying to explain their suicidal behaviour, some said they just couldn't live with their memories and that the only way to get rid of the body that had provoked the abuse, and still bore the scars, was to kill it. Suicide may also appeal as a way of ending the unbearable aftermath of abuse. It seems that the more often a boy is abused or the greater the number of abusers, the more marked is the tendency towards suicide.

From Attachment to Hatred

When a youngster is being abused by a close relative, the boy experiences great emotional confusion. He loves his aggressor, whether it be his father, his brother, or his uncle, who is at last paying him attention, but he simultaneously detests him because he is using him, using his body, and abusing his sense of trust and his innocence. The abused child becomes perturbed, unable to sort out these contradictory emotions. He can thus end up thinking or doing one thing and its opposite all at the same time. He may for example make a complaint against his aggressor while continuing to see him in secret; or he may blame himself for going along with the abuser while continuing to meet his demands.

The victim's extreme emotional confusion is often such that he cannot tell whether he should still love the man who from time to time, however briefly, showed him affection, paid him attention, or lavished favours on him, or whether he should hate him. Thus it is that Pascal still refuses to reveal the identity of the person who abused his trust; that Bruno refuses to bear witness against his stepfather; that Martin and James consider they merely paid back a debt in surrendering themselves to those who took them in when they had run away. In these cases, as in many others, the ex-victims fluctuate between feelings of anger and compassion, between wanting vengeance and not wanting to harm a man "who was a good person apart from that" or "who has since reformed his life."

It is not easy for a child or a young adolescent to turn against someone he has previously loved and who has sometimes been a role model for him. If it is difficult to forget a stranger who has hurt you and left you with bad memories that still haunt you, then how is it possible to forget a father, brother, uncle or close friend? Whether the boy wants it or not, a father or a brother will thus always continue to be a part of the young man's life. At the very least he will always hear others speak of him, even if he doesn't see him any more.

Rarely is an aggressor just simply that for the child, who often retains some good memories of the person who abused him. Hence the child's difficulty in knowing whether he hates or loves this person, feels attached to him, or is indifferent towards him. The little attentions the child received within the context of his abuse – the kind words, the small favours, the gifts, etc. – may at some point mitigate its negative or traumatizing aspects. The same goes for the feared consequences of disclosing the abuse: the caring the child has felt may make him hesitate. What will happen to the person who is to be denounced? The child generally asks himself: "What do I have to gain from it? What do I have to lose if I denounce my father, my brother, my uncle, or my friend?" Cases of incest are particularly dramatic. Not only does the young person risk losing a big brother, a father, or a grandfather: he risks losing his whole family. In fact, often the only ones "punished" for what has happened are the victims. They are taken out of their family milieu and have barely any contact with their family of origin from then on.

The extent of the child's confusion and his feeling of having been betrayed will obviously depend upon the relationship of trust that was previously established between the boy and his abuser. Repetition of the abuse or the involvement of several aggressors will obviously worsen the situation. Paul, Justin, Oliver, Maxim, and Eric, who were all abused by several men, appeared to be the most crippled and the most fragile as a result of their past experiences: each of them has attempted suicide more than once; each of them has been seriously involved with drugs and alcohol since earliest adolescence, and they all manifest serious emotional and sexual problems. They have hardly any markers to guide their way on an emotional level and have no references to gauge their own feelings or those of others. Their emotional disarray is enormous.

Most of these boys will take the journey from affection to hatred, but most of the time they will feel ambivalent towards their abusers. Nobody is completely good or completely bad, totally in one category or the other. Some young boys will, to the same extent if not more so, strongly resent their family or the social services workers who failed to believe them, protect them, or help them. It is not a simple matter to disown a father, brother, uncle, or friend in whom total trust has earlier been invested. It is not easy, either, to live with feelings of hatred. As one young adult put it: "With hatred, you end up destroying yourself."

Pain and Pleasure

In an abusive situation the physical sensations experienced by the boy may be at odds with the reality of abuse. The body may register pleasure – have an erection or ejaculate – while reason refuses such a response, is astonished by it, or quite plainly disgusted by it. This type of split between body and mind could also explain a boy's attempts to punish his body for what it felt or to "harden" it so that it no longer feels anything. The same can be said for the overconsumption of drugs, medications, or alcohol so often seen in ex-victims of sexual abuse: it is an attempt to anaesthetize feeling.

To have felt something that, at the time or in retrospect, seems like sexual pleasure is invariably interpreted by the boy as proof that the abuse is perhaps not truly abuse and that he did, to a degree, consent to it. It cannot be repeated too often: one must never make the mistake of believing that an erection or ejaculation signifies consent, even satisfaction; nor must one confuse a certain receptivity with consent. Some boys, at the time they are being abused, have been so deprived of affection that they would spontaneously accept any physical attention, no matter what its source.

Nevertheless, many boys interpret their physical reactions to being caressed as an obvious sign of voluntary participation. "If my body reacted, if I felt a certain pleasure, that means it wasn't really a question of abuse" is how they tend to reason, at least to begin with. Numerous survivors of abuse have spoken of the physical, psychological, and emotional rewards they obtained through their abuse. Not only did they experience excitement, erection, and ejaculation but they felt recognized, important, even loved. Their ambivalence as to whether they were suffering or simply receiving pleasure is understandable. They felt both, in different parts of themselves.

The experience of physical or sexual gratification during abuse leaves victims perplexed and uneasy. How can acts that disgust them or cause them to suffer be a source of pleasure? Doesn't that prove they have something to reproach themselves for? No. Pain and pleasure are not necessarily contradictory, and sexuality is one of the areas where they can coexist. Andrew, speaking eloquently of this, describes the excruciating pain inflicted on him when his father sodomized him, but he also describes his simultaneous discovery of erotic sensations.

Let us not forget that it is through sexual abuse that many of these boys discovered the typically masculine physiological reactions: erogenous zones, erections, ejaculation, whether their own or those of the aggressor. "Whether or not you want to, you get pleasure out of it somewhere," said Francis, victim of father-son incest. "Somewhere inside, I liked it," confirms Anthony, also perplexed, talking about the sexual touching by an older boy who was his neighbour. How can they distinguish thereafter between abuse and what might be considered "normal"? How can they integrate the terrible impression of having "felt something" on a sexual level with an involvement that is perceived as being offensive? Is it possible to feel simultaneously molested and physically gratified? It seems crazy. But it is precisely such perplexity and uneasiness that an aggressor counts on.

In his study of sexual abusers, Nicolas Groth[3] emphasizes that aggressors make a substantial effort to have their young male victims experience sexual excitation or orgasm. Such an effort has many goals. When the victim connects his sexual excitement with consensual participation, he feels all the more guilty or confused and will be discouraged from making a complaint. He is also afraid that his testimony will be discredited, to the benefit of the abuser. If it is really about abuse, how can the boy have felt any gratification? This is the question certain parents, police, social workers, judges, or lawyers will ask themselves. Groth[4] explains that people wrongly believe that if a man is in a state of fear or anxiety, he will not be able to have an erection or to ejaculate; moreover, in confounding ejaculation and orgasm, the victim himself may not understand his own physiological responses and may thus begin to doubt his own sexuality. To the abuser, ejaculation by his victim would signify that he had won complete control over the child's body. This apparent enjoyment confirms his fantasy that the boy has more or less consciously provoked what has happened, even perhaps wished for it.

The young person's interpretation of his own reactions, physical or emotional, is of the utmost importance. How can one hope that this interpretation will be subtle enough when even adults find it difficult to separate gratification and participation, excitement and desire, ejaculation and pleasure? To feel himself divided and torn between love and hatred, desire and disgust, pleasure and pain is not helpful to a young person who is only just beginning to discover sexuality. He is caught in a torrent of contradictory emotions and feelings in which answers to his questions are impossible to find.

Loyalty or Betrayal?

The boy vacillates between a desire to put an end to distressing acts and a fear of appearing ungrateful towards someone who has, in many instances, given him something. Revealing the abuse is all the more difficult for a child or adolescent if in the past he has viewed the aggressor as a significant other. This ambiguity creates guilt when the situation is disclosed and the aggressor confronted. One might even say that the boys hesitate to reveal what has happened to them because of a certain masculine solidarity. Some of them will never reveal the identity of the man who abused them, as if such a thing were "not done" and as if the bond between them were, in spite of everything, stronger than reason, stronger than the law, more important even than the suffering of the victim.

The misgivings surrounding the masculine experience of sexual abuse do nothing to diminish the boys' confusion. Some will only with difficulty be able to dissociate sexual abuse from homosexual initiation. Thus, a boy who sees himself as homosexual or bisexual will have even more difficulty in divulging the abuse he has endured. On the one hand, he will be afraid others may think that he invited these contacts, since he is assumed to be drawn towards sexual relations between men. On the other hand, he will be afraid of unjustly heaping abuse on an older person who has, in a certain way, initiated him sexually and allowed him, perhaps, to discover the "real nature" of his sexual orientation.

Abuse puts its victims in a double bind. Either a boy keeps his mouth shut and continues to put up with the sexual abuse he wants to bring an end to, or he speaks up and, in so doing, not only brings down on himself the wrath and the resentment of someone he feels close to but also offends and antagonizes others who are close to the aggressor. This hesitation between keeping the secret versus committing a betrayal persists because basic questions in the mind of the child or adolescent have yet to be answered: Why did it happen? What part did I play in my "seduction"? If I didn't speak up about it until now, why do it now? Why would I attack a man who is my father/my uncle/my friend? Why didn't I stand up for myself, defend myself? Do I really need others to sort this out?

Disclosing the abuse, when it is done, does not necessarily resolve the victim's ambivalence. Far from it. Denunciation may increase feelings of anguish and guilt and reinforce the fear of rejection and losing the family's affection for ever, the aggressor more often than not being part of the immediate family or entourage. The victim's fear that, in breaking the secret of the abuse, he will be breaking an unwritten contract must not be underestimated. In cases where testimony against the abuser is required, the boy's reticence is sometimes clear, as James's testimony illustrates:

The man we're talking about – my friends introduced me to him so he could put me up whenever I ran away from the group home. For an old guy, he seemed quite cool. He gradually began feeling me up. I let him get on with it because I didn't think he would go any further: he knew I had a girlfriend. One morning, when I woke up, I saw he was sleeping beside me and I asked myself some questions. I had smoked quite a bit of hash the evening before so I wasn't in a state to do anything about it … At the time, anyway, I couldn't care less about anything.

Afterwards, it became more or less habitual for him. I went along with it for the sake of peace and quiet. And another thing, I didn't have

anywhere else to go. I told myself: "It's my life, it's the life I've chosen."
I was agreeable to a certain point because I wanted to stay there. When
we got up, it was as though nothing had happened. It wasn't rape. I
didn't see it as rape. He did it with other fellows, but I wasn't aware of
that at the time. He gave me the key to his apartment and I could invite
my girlfriend if I was alone.

It was when the police came to school to question me that the affair
took another turn. The police told me the old man was putting young
boys in touch with other men who wanted sex with them. At that point,
it hadn't got that far with me. The police said they wouldn't let me go
if I didn't talk. It took a few hours before I capitulated. They took me
out of school for a while so as not to prejudice the enquiry, because there
were other boys at my school who were involved. The only person I
agreed to talk to about it was an educator who had been a victim of
abuse himself when he was young. He understood me, he really did.

I went to court and testified. Going to court was a picnic. We waited
around, and then in the end there was no need to testify since he had
pleaded guilty. That was okay by me. The only thing that still bothers
me is that each time I do drugs it reminds me of all that again. I don't
know if I've really got it in for him. Some of the people I know are saying
that he got off too easily because he only got a few weekends in prison.
As for me, I say to myself: After all, if it happened, it just had to happen.
Maybe that's why I'm no longer bothered by it. It's as though it didn't
happen to me. It's passed. It's finished. That's all. I needed him, and he
needed me. He didn't turn me in when I was a runaway. Why did I have
to denounce him?

Incapable of Loving, Incapable of Being Loved

This phrase, from the story told by Andrew who was sexually
abused by his father at the age of thirteen, shows the confusion
of a child whose experience of abuse has clouded the usual cognitive references regarding love and sexuality. Often, having had
no experience of empathetic or protective adults – on the contrary,
having experienced the imposition of sexuality – some ex-victims
will find themselves without or almost without the ability to
express themselves emotionally in matters of love or sex. Mirror-
ing what they have lived, the sexuality of such men becomes
simply a matter of power relationships, based on their impression
that if they do not exert control over others, those others will make

use of them. This explains why some men change from victims into dominant types, even if they do not go so far as to commit aggressions. Many respondents describe how much they detest it when their partner takes the initiative during sexual relations, as their abuser used to do. Sexual partners who assert themselves may seem to be potential aggressors.

Since most ex-victims have not learned to communicate or to affirm their real needs or emotions or their true feelings, their experiences in love are all the more difficult. Being abused has prevented the child from developing the capacity to express himself and encouraged him to remain silent about what he is feeling. To protect himself against others and to anaesthetize his pain, the boy may go on to more or less consciously detach himself to some extent from reality. Alcohol or drugs are often used to induce a state of numbness, fostering the impression that he is not quite present in reality, that he is somewhat of a "zombie." He functions, but awareness seems to be lacking.

The conviction that they are not worth loving is forcibly expressed in the stories told by child victims of sexual abuse. It even becomes a self-fulfilling prophecy. Indeed, these young men can be brought by their low self-esteem to avoid or to sabotage relationships with significant others or to develop strong emotional or sexual dependencies. This avoidance is caused by fear of suffering or of being once again exploited in the context of an intimate relationship. The reaction of dependence is without doubt caused by both the fear of losing an unmerited love and by a preexisting emotional deficiency that has been reinforced by the abuse. Each case gives the impression that a vast gulf, impossible to bridge, exists between the victim of sexual abuse and his present partner. These men have an insatiable desire for attention, affection, or gratification that no relationship can satisfy.

The sense that they have been soiled for ever reinforces, in some victims, the feeling of being unworthy. Self-disgust or an aversion to physical contact hardly disposes them towards harmonious affectionate or sexual relationships. When abuse has invoked cognitive association between suffering and pleasure, pain and sexuality, humiliation and eroticism, the young man may conclude that he is not normal and never will be. From this belief to the conviction that he is not worth loving is only one small step.

A great timidity towards girls or women often appears in young male victims of heterosexual or bisexual orientation. They fear that, during sexual relations, the girls will discover their secret and their supposed "deviance." The fear that their sexual behaviour will reveal their past can impose a temporary celibacy. The fear of becoming attached also plays a part, love being associated with future deception or suffering – which cannot fail to bring instability into a loving relationship. Among the men interviewed, failed couple relationships were common. Such failures sometimes arise from chronic sexual dissatisfaction, whatever form it may take.

The intrusive thoughts that sometimes surface during sexual relations, particularly memories of the abuse, diminish or destroy whatever satisfaction the ex-victim might experience. "It comes back to me even when I don't want to think about it, when it isn't the right time, for example when I want to sleep, when I'm making love, when I'm masturbating. That's the worst because I'm playing with a penis and it makes me think of his. I find that disgusting – a penis," said one respondent. Such a reaction is not out of the ordinary. According to author-therapist Mic Hunter, more than eighty percent of male victims of incest report having flashbacks of the incest when they are making love.[5] These men are dealing with cognitive associations between touching, stroking, sexuality and abuse of power, fear, shame, or even physical pain. Being touched means being abused, affection signifies sexuality, physical closeness is equated with promiscuity. Even in a situation that does not objectively present any danger, the ex-victim will remain distrustful and aloof: "If someone is good to me, I tell myself that he must want something in return, that I will have to pay for it sooner or later"; "When someone seems interested in me, I'm on my guard. I take off because I never know what it might lead to."

Since the connection to self, as well as to others, has been disturbed by the abuse, it follows that all relationships with others will be insidiously poisoned. This goes for close relationships as well as for those with strangers. Both are coloured by fear of abuse and the distrust that results from it. Once deceived by a family member, a young boy or an adolescent male easily comes to the idea that everyone can do the same thing: everyone becomes a

potential rapist in his eyes, both men and women. Any relationship is threatening. The fear that his trust will again be betrayed
engenders a wariness that can come close to paranoia, and that
feeds on itself. This distrust shows up most clearly as a reluctance
to accept sympathy or affection, especially if expressed physically,
as if love or compassion inevitably hid something ugly.

Ex-victims of abuse often have difficulty believing in relationships that are transparent, sincere, and empathic. Some of them
have come to believe that no one could ever love them, only their
bodies. As a result, they will overvalue the parts of their anatomy
that drew the most attention from their abuser. It wasn't he himself that was loved, the young man will say, but his thighs, his
penis, his abdomen, his torso, his soft skin, his hair, his smooth,
beardless face, etc. Consequently he believes that, if he wants to
be loved again, he must show off those same attributes. Some
young men recognize and deplore this dynamic even as they perpetuate it. For such young men, sexuality is solely an instrument
to be used for their own ends. This at least is the lesson they have
retained. Several ex-victims of abuse make no bones about their
efforts to manipulate others with sex. Have they not learned that
those older than they are, or adults, can be thus inveigled and
that their only power lies in their capacity to seduce? This perception can translate into inappropriate sexualization of relationships with others through exhibitionist behaviour and, sometimes,
prostitution. Experiences of this sort will not fail to confirm to the
young men that the conclusions they had initially drawn from
being sexually abused were correct: the only reason they are
"loved" is for sex.

Trying to Forget ... When the Body Refuses to Be Hushed

Even when you try to suppress it, the body and the memory insist on
remembering. In particular, boys who have been repeatedly abused
will have so integrated certain images, certain fears, and certain
reflexes that, many years later, physical or psychosomatic after-effects
of their abuse will make themselves felt. Such symptoms include:

– Difficulty or inability to relax or to sleep. Numerous respondents testify that their sleep is irregular, troubled, or disturbed
   by nightmares.

- Hypervigilance: This brings about difficulty not only in the person's abandoning himself to sleep but in his being constantly on the lookout for dangers that, in most cases, no longer exist. For example, some men fear, fifteen years later, that the aggressor will break into their house at night to rape or kill them. Even if they know this irrational idea makes no sense, they cannot shake it off.
- A large variety of physical discomforts of psychosomatic origin, such as nausea associated with the idea of sex, even when the ex-victim is involved sexually with a person he loves and desires; enuresis, or involuntary defecation, in situations that remind them of the abuse.
- Hyperconsciousness of their physical appearance and of being looked at by others, whether this is used to seduce another or to repulse a potential aggressor.
- Sexual dysfunctions ranging from loss of interest in sex to a compulsive sexuality. What was formerly traumatising may apparently be transformed into pleasure, as if the person wanted to convince himself there is nothing frightening in sexuality. (On the contrary, it is proven that there is much to be afraid of.)
- Claustrophobia (or fear of being confined against the will or of being held prisoner).
- A persistent anxiety and anguish even when it appears that all is well or panic and loss of control, even violence, if a situation is viewed as an aggression.

Contrary to these obviously harmful symptoms, other reactions may be considered as "solutions" or defence mechanisms, if not flights from reality. In order to get over the pain and repetition of the abuse, the child, adolescent, or young adult will more or less consciously try to forget the events. Here we find:

- Total or partial, permanent or temporary amnesia concerning the abuse, or some of its elements, or even the stage of childhood in which it happened. Keeping the traumatism in the memory would seem to be too painful. This reaction explains why numerous boy victims of sexual aggression may, for a long time, seem asymptomatic. Their traumatisms are well and truly present but in some way quiescent.
- Abuse of medication, drugs, or alcohol. This constitutes for many a way to escape from reality, a preferred way to freeze

one's emotions. Flight from reality is, if not typical, at least very common. According to Mezey and King, clinical studies are unanimous in reporting toxic substance abuse in males who have been sexually abused.[6] At least sixty percent of the men in detox appear to have been sexually abused, according to one specialist.[7] Workers in the field of toxicology confirm more and more the correlation between previous abuse and present dependence in a large number of the men they treat.

– The denial or minimizing of the abuse itself or of its consequences. In such cases, the victim himself hesitates to recognize the truth, and this is apparent in his doubts about the quality of his memory: "Did I really go through that?" some respondents will ask themselves at one point or another. The possible existence of "false memory" emphasized recently by psychiatrists and American parent groups[8] does not help to clarify the situation (although I would estimate, with others, that cases of "false memory" are quite limited when compared with situations of actual abuse that are frequently denied).

The confusions, paradoxes, and problems pointed out in this chapter throw some light on the negative repercussions of the sexual abuse of young boys. Cases with less injurious effects may also exist. On this point, some respondents made reference to the ease with which they can create or sublimate, in music, painting, or poetry for example, a faculty they accord to past traumatisms. Others indicated a more positive integration of past traumatic experiences, which they regard as learning experiences that help them to manage other difficult situations in their lives – if only by being more assertive and less naïve. In other words, as one respondent said, it is possible "to do more with less," and the interminable list of after-effects of sexual abuse does not preclude the possibility that victims may emerge, in the end, with greater strength.

DENNIS'S STORY

Dennis, thirty-one years old, was abused when he was eight.

Before it happened, I was an athletic little kid, very lively. I was born into an ordinary family: good parents, three brothers and a sister. The sexual abuse was the first thing that changed my life.

It happened with the man who looked after the outside skating rink in the park opposite our house. In the winter, I often went there to play hockey. I knew him well. He was in his forties. He began by inviting two of my friends and myself to his home. At the beginning, nothing out of the ordinary happened. We talked, we had fun. There were lots of games in the house. One day, I found myself alone with him. He offered to give me a massage because I had a sore back. I accepted. I remember feeling a bit odd about it. Actually I did have some idea of what could happen, but I wasn't certain. He began with a proper massage. I was just in my underwear. Then he went lower down – the touching became sexual.

I went along with it out of curiosity. There was no violence, I wasn't forced. It happened three or four times, in the same way. It was later that things got worse. When he asked for, when he insisted on, more than touching and masturbation, I didn't want to. He didn't threaten me, but I quickly left his place and went home, intending not go to back. A short time after that, I didn't see him around any more. He just disappeared. I think he was probably doing the same thing with other young boys. I've never said anything to anyone about it, except my wife, and that was only a few years ago.

After the last occasion, I began to be afraid: afraid of running into him by accident; afraid he might use force to get me to his home. I didn't dare go anywhere near the skating rink until he moved away. And then I felt guilty, towards my parents mostly, for not having said anything to them.

When I was getting on for ten, I did things with my little cousin who was seven years old. I told him what to do to me. I didn't force him. This happened a few times, until he asked me to stop, because I wanted to go further – like the guy at the skating rink. Neither of us ever spoke about it again, though we did almost do it once, I think. But he ran off. I don't know if he

hates me for it. I have the impression he feels just as awkward
about it as I do. There is still some unfinished business between
us, even twenty years later. While it was happening, I was
imagining I was reliving the experience I had gone through, but
in reverse. I was telling the other guy what to do. It's like a
wound but it's also pleasurable. It's strange. I ask myself today
if my cousin has suffered as much as I had, after what we did
together, and if he too was confused afterwards ... I can't tell if
it was really abusive, what I did ...

My first sexual fantasies revolved around boys my own age,
maybe a bit older or bit younger. With my cousin, it happened
because he was there, accessible. I found it exciting to look, to
touch parts of his body, but it was also exciting because it was
forbidden. I used to ask myself why I wasn't doing it with
females, why it was always males. All around me, the others
were talking about their sexual encounters with girls. But
I hadn't had any at the time. This was reinforcing my fear
I might be homosexual.

Some time later, I had sex with some of the players on my
hockey team, boys my own age. There was one in particular
who invited me all the time to go and sleep at his place. This
led me to question whether I wasn't homosexual. I was about
eleven or twelve. I found it difficult to approach girls. I was
embarrassed. I felt more at ease with another boy. My first
sexual experiences had been like that. It went on for two years.
I often had relations with the same boys. Afterwards, I tried
hard to get oriented towards women, to go out with girls, to go
dancing, for example.

At fifteen, I met the girl who would become my wife. We
stayed together fifteen years – up until last summer. At that
point it was clear I wasn't interested in homosexuality any
more. I only valued women. I was telling myself that what was
past was past. The friend I was getting it off with most often
became jealous. I got mad with him at the time and dropped
out of the hockey team because of that. It was quite a bit later
that I realized I was still having homosexual fantasies in spite
of everything. As for my wife, it took a long time before we
had sexual relations. I was awkward, ill at ease. At least ten
months went by before we had sex. I was afraid she would

discover my past history, that she would sense it, that she would be able to figure it out. I only spoke to her years later about it.

I had started doing drugs when I was thirteen years old. I don't think there was any direct link with the abuse. Maybe it had more to do with my lack of self-assurance? I smoked pot, did hash, and drank alcohol. I did it just to try it, but the more I did it, the more I liked it, because it also helped me to feel less shy. It made me feel superior, not inferior as I had felt before.

I used to feel ill at ease with my parents too, because of all the secrets, because of my guilt and the remorse for the abuse of my little cousin. I was carrying all that guilt alone. That's still the grossest thing, even today, having abused someone – more than the abuse I went through myself.

Deep down inside I still feel aggressive towards the type who made use of me. If I met him today I don't know what I would do. I would treat him like the scum of the earth. I trusted him – to begin with. Afterwards, I couldn't bring myself to trust any adult. I was always on guard, imagined all sorts of things about men. When a man paid attention to me, especially in hockey, I became somewhat paranoid.

I decided to play macho to fool others. I was trying to convince myself, too. I often asked myself why he had abused me rather than someone else. This paranoia is still with me. I'm always asking myself, even today, if people think I'm a homo. Especially with girls, I feel on the defensive.

By the time my early married life had all but removed the homosexual fantasies from my mind, they resurfaced. I was around nineteen or twenty years old. It was as though, once the "love at first sight" phase was over, I began again to look elsewhere, but I was only interested in guys, as I had been before. But my fantasies never became a reality. I wanted to go ahead but always drew back at the last moment. I saw homosexuality as something bad, not normal. Sex with my wife was going quite well. She wasn't aware of anything. To begin with, I was embarrassed inside. I was afraid I wouldn't know what to do. Finally, I got used to it. Perhaps I stopped myself approaching other women because I didn't think I was good enough. I felt different from others. I felt ignorant – especially because at

home, we had never talked about sex. My parents worked hard,
they were busy from morning till night. No one had time to
talk about that. I was always scared of disappointing a woman.
   At one point I was afraid of becoming an abuser. I feel less
afraid of that now. It was mainly when I had my daughter, who
is almost four years old now, that the thought of it plagued me.
I didn't even want to change her diaper; I was too afraid I'd get
ideas. I stayed away from her. And yet, I must say I had no
idea in my head about abusing her. I was just dreadfully afraid
of getting the idea. As time passed, my fears disappeared. In
any case, since my divorce I hardly see my daughter any more.
   My aggressivity, my being ill at ease? I was on drugs when
I went through all that. I first went for therapy a few years ago,
but I didn't talk about what had happened when I was little. It
was after having given vent to everything else that I ended up
telling myself I must grapple with my history of sexual abuse
as well. I was more or less ready to do it. I was very afraid of
being judged by others. I hesitated just as I was going to begin
opening up about it. I was finding it too distressing. I took off,
abandoned my therapy. It was only recently that I spoke about
it to my present therapist, hardly a month ago. I felt I no longer
had any choice about being honest or dishonest with myself.
I didn't want to avoid my problems any longer. My abuse, my
fantasies, and everything that I don't accept in all that play a
part in my doing drugs. In the beginning, doing drugs was just
for pleasure, but then I realized that it allowed me to escape my
problems. You can imagine the rest.
   When I finally spoke up about the abuse I had gone through,
I was accepted. It surprised me and I felt heartened. In my ex-
druggie group, I met several guys who had also been abused,
who had even been in prostitution afterwards. And I had been
so sure that I was a rare case ...
   About a dozen years ago, I read in a newspaper that the man
who had abused me had been arrested, but it was in a different region to the one where I had known him. I was pleased
that he was living in another area. I was relieved to realize
I would never have to testify against him. I could never have
told my story in front of everyone because I don't want to be
judged. It seems good to me, just the same, to condemn men
who abuse children. In therapy, I met a guy who had abused

his own children. I took it like a fist in my gut. I was winded. My little daughter came into my mind right away.

Before, I didn't so much see what had happened to me as an abuse. I considered it to be a homosexual relationship between an adult and a child. It's only recently that I've come to see it as abusive, even if it wasn't violent. I myself more or less consented. That's what made me feel guilty more than anything else. I was only a child. I bear him a grudge now. That probably signifies that it really was abuse. He made use of me. However, it's maybe less the abuse part of it than the homosexual part of it that affected me most in the end. I've never felt okay about that ...

When I had homosexual fantasies I couldn't control, I had the idea of hiring a male prostitute. At night, I would cruise the streets where they hang out. A prostitute was a better solution, less distressing for me. The prostitute was okay with it and after, for me it was out of sight, out of mind. I wasn't accountable to anybody.

In the end, I had a relationship with a fellow my own age. He was the initiator. We were both on drugs. We saw each other two or three more times. We worked together, but a short while later he was transferred to another town. He was married too, as I was. It was sex pure and simple for both of us. We never spoke of it. We did it, that's all, when the occasion presented itself. I think he was even more ill at ease with it than I was.

Today I have fantasies about older men. I let them dominate me. Just in my head. But since I left my wife, I'm thinking seriously about it. Should I try and realize these fantasies? If it would help me get over it, I would. If by doing it I could really know who I am and what I want, I would do it. For years now, I've been asking myself the same question: Am I homosexual, heterosexual, or bisexual?

FRANCIS'S STORY

Francis, seventeen, was a victim of father-son incest from twelve to sixteen years of age.

I'm an only child. I never got along well with my father. I got along better with my mother. My father is an army man and that sort of mentality ruled the household: no going out after eight o'clock in the evening, no visiting friends. There was no possibility of discussing anything with him. We hardly spoke to one another.

I was twelve when he began touching my bum as I got out of the shower. At first, it was when I had a towel around me. He had never before been affectionate with me. I told myself that's what it was. It seemed quite normal. But when he began taking off the towel and pawing my butt, I knew something was wrong. I felt hurt. My eyes filled with tears whenever he did it and I would take off to my room.

I asked myself if he did it to show that he loved me or if it was something else. Maybe my father had problems. I didn't know what to think. On the one hand, I told myself it was good that he was beginning to pay attention to me, to be affectionate. I figured I'd enjoy it, go along with it, and that maybe it was just because he loved me. He used to say he liked stroking me because I had soft skin. But then things turned different. At one point he grabbed my penis and pulled me against him. I was quite naked. When my mother had gone out, he took me into his bedroom. He lay down on top of me. It went as far as ejaculation. He masturbated me, asked me to masturbate him, to put my hands on his bum and squeeze hard. At that point I just didn't understand it any more. I didn't know how to react. Should I let him go on doing it or should I speak out? I was afraid of how he'd react if I denounced him.

I really began to understand that something was wrong when I saw the film *My Body Is My Body*. I understood what was going on: what my father was doing with me wasn't right, I told myself. For quite a while, my father had been coming into the bathroom and looking at me in the shower or in the bath, but before he had never touched me. I would turn so he could only see me from the back. When I became an adolescent it began to upset me but I didn't say anything because I was afraid of him.

When I watched the erotic movies we had at home, or the ones on television, I could see that it was always a man and a woman and not two men together. I knew there was a problem somewhere with my father. I began to have problems, to become introverted, to drink, to take drugs secretly, to act out, like breaking window panes, stealing, setting fires, getting into fights. That's why I ended up in a group home.

Sexual relations with my father happened often: once or twice a week, when I was alone with him at home. It had become an exchange of favours: he was giving me money in return. When he didn't give me any money, I helped myself from his wallet. He must have noticed it but he acted as if it didn't matter. For me, having the money seemed to reduce the pain. With time, it almost became normal for me. I got some sort of pleasure out of it, got an erection, even ejaculated, and one half of me was okay with it all. For my body, it had become a habit. But it wasn't okay in my mind.

Once I asked my father why he did that to me? He replied: "I already told you. It's because you have soft skin. It's stronger than I am. And, apart from that, your mother doesn't give me enough sex." I spoke to my mother about it. She didn't take me seriously, but she said: "Okay, so I'll give him more sex." She never spoke about it again. That did something to me. There was my mother, who was supposed to protect me, doing absolutely nothing about it. From then on I started doing drugs.

Around the age of fourteen or fifteen, I said to myself: What am I going to do with my life? I have to make a future for myself. I can't always be my father's slave. I ran away, and took as many drugs as I could buy. I was stoned eighteen hours a day. I skipped school, I had trouble relating to girls and I changed girlfriends often. The first girl I became attached to dropped me: I saw that as another form of abuse. I felt betrayed, like with my father. I didn't like that feeling but I continued to go out with girls, one after the other. Each time I went out with a girl I had to have sex. I had to prove something, that I wasn't a fag, I wasn't a homosexual. I made love even when I didn't feel right with a girl, just because I was trying to prove something to myself. I'm afraid of being gay.

I'm afraid of being an abuser too. You hear it all the time: "He who has been abused will abuse."

During the time I was having sex with my father, I stayed away from my girlfriend. The two things at the same time didn't seem right. It's very different, penetrating a woman and penetrating a man or being penetrated by a man. With a woman, it's normal, it's more comfortable – it's great, wouldn't you agree? With my father, I had to be on all fours so he could penetrate me. It was humiliating. It hurt. I used to bite the pillow. Even when I was totally stoned I felt the pain. Once he asked me to penetrate him, and that disgusted me the most. I ran to clean myself up right away afterwards. I took off through the bathroom window. I got completely stoned that night.

When I wore shorts or walked about in a dressing gown, he would say I was provoking him sexually. That made me mad and I would change my clothes. Finally I was so afraid of turning him on that I wore two of everything: two pairs of underpants, two pairs of socks, two shirts. Even in summer, I would wear several layers of clothing and a belt with a padlock. I also put padlocks on my boots – my Doc Martens. That way, even if he could get my pants down, he couldn't get my boots off.

When I started taking girls home, or receiving calls from my girlfriends, he behaved stupidly. He would lecture me: I wasn't allowed to hold their hand or touch them, never mind kiss them, in front of my father. It was easier to go to their place than to take them home. In the beginning, when he and I were making out, he used to say to me: "This will show you how: you'll see, with a woman it's even better." But he was jealous. He wanted to prevent me making love with girls. One time he said to me: "I forbid you to make love before you're married." I told him he couldn't give me orders, considering what he himself was doing. He got annoyed. Fortunately, some friends just happened to drop by to pick me up, otherwise there would have been quite a brawl.

Often, when I was making out with a girlfriend, I would have flashbacks. I could see my father on the wall of the bedroom. When I'm drinking, when I've taken drugs and I get close to a bed, I still have this type of flashback: I can see my father again, as if he's there. I associate drink, drugs, and a bed with abuse. It all goes together in my mind. Sometimes, when

I'm making love, I freeze up because I can see my father again, and I can see myself with him. When this happens, I leap out of bed right away; I have to get drunk or take a lot of drugs to numb my mind.

When I make love with the girl I'm in love with now, in spite of myself I find myself doing things I did with my father. I squeeze her buttocks very hard. She says I'm hurting her sometimes. I know it, but it's like, having learned it, I can't stop doing it. On the other hand, there are some positions, sexual positions, that remind me too much of my father. I just can't do it. There are only two positions where I can go ahead with no holds barred so to speak, because these positions don't work with two men. If I think about the abuse, for sure I'll lose my erection. It takes me about an hour, at least, to get it up again. For example, blowing in my ear, that used to get me interested. My father often did it to me because he had discovered it turned me on. My present girlfriend began doing it without being aware. It paralyzed me. I warned her. If she forgets, I just freeze. I lose interest in sex right away. Another example: when my girlfriend begins stroking me, I ask myself what she's after. It reminds me of my father who always stroked me when he wanted sex.

My fantasy life is affected by my past too. Sometimes it happens that I think of overpowering a girl and taking her by force. Then again, I like making love on the spur of the moment. It's like a challenge. I wonder how the person will react. The other night, my girlfriend and I made out in front of one of her girlfriends who had never seen that before. We were partially hidden by the sheets. The friend looked inside to see if it was really true – if we weren't just teasing her. It would be more difficult for me to do that in front of a guy, especially if I knew him. With men I'm more reserved. In my therapy group, that was the first time I ever cried in front of other men. Sometimes I imagine a threesome, preferably two girls and myself, or two guys and a girl. I did it once, with a fellow I knew who had also been abused. It only lasted fifteen minutes. We were both too nervous. It was better in fantasy than in reality. Sometimes I imagine two men are making love. They are my age or a bit older. The guys I'm attracted to aren't like my father. They're not hypocritical, they're not secretive. I prefer to see

two homos embracing each other than to know a grown man is
abusing a young person. But I prefer women, whether they're
young or old, that's for sure.

I have difficulties with homos. One evening last year, with
some friends, we were in Montreal's gay village. I spoke to one
of them, enticed him into a back lane, and then, with my chums
who were waiting, we went through his pockets and tried to
rub his nose in the sidewalk. It was like getting revenge. The
last person I did that to was a cousin of one of the guys in the
group home. We went to his place and robbed him. Afterwards, I thought it over and decided I wouldn't do that any
more. I even looked him up and told him I was sorry. When he
asked me why I'd done it, I told him what had happened to
me. He understood and forgave me. He encouraged me to
make a complaint against my father. After all, it's guys like my
father I've got it in for, not homosexuals. Today I can make
the distinction between hypocrites who abuse children and
homosexuals.

After I went into the group home, I denounced my father.
The educators were wondering why I didn't want to leave the
group home and visit my family, especially at times when
I knew I would be alone with my father. Once, when my
mother had come to pick me up and I had refused to come out
of my room, she got really pissed off. The educators asked me
why I didn't want to go with her. I blurted out: "Because my
father abuses me!" They began legal procedures. But my father
was acquitted for lack of evidence. It was all done very fast;
I wasn't even able to speak with my lawyer to prepare myself.
In court my father said nothing, made no plea. I made a complaint against the lawyer and I want to appeal the decision
because of the way the process was handled. Not being
believed has left its mark. I was nothing but a kid who was
already showing signs of having serious problems and was now
bringing a complaint against his very respectable father! They
never believe young people. I lost confidence in the system.
When I first went out from the group home, I began taking
coke again; seeing him acquitted like that was like being abused
all over again.

Doing drugs has become automatic for me. Whenever I have
the slightest problem, the smallest upset, I have to take drugs to

relax. If not, I get depressed, and I start thinking about suicide.
I'm not brave enough to slit my wrists, but I've mutilated
myself sometimes. I cut my arms. It used to happen when I had
bad trips. The same nightmare always went with it: I had to
escape so my father wouldn't corner me; I had to get to another
world. I threw myself into the traffic once; tried to hang myself
too, but the rope broke.

Talking about the abuse I've gone through has brought me
some relief. I've been in therapy groups. Now I know I'm not
the only boy that's been abused. That's helped a bit. The group
home is my family. I'm leaving in a few days and it's difficult
for me. When they told me I was going to leave, I broke down,
sobbing. I'd never cried so much. Now it's up to me to make
my own family.

I've got myself a new sweetheart and this time it's serious,
even if she was only fourteen years old when we first met.
She's just turned fifteen. It was weird, the way we met. One
evening, I was walking through a park and I heard screams.
She was on the point of being raped by a gang of young men.
I identified right away with what was happening to her and
chased the attackers. Although I wasn't able to catch them, she
sees me as a hero for having saved her. But I don't want her to
see me as a hero: I did for her what I would have wanted
someone to do for me. Being with her has allowed me to start
over again from scratch. I want to start a family with her. She
was pregnant, but she's just had a miscarriage. When I'm in
love, I'm possessive, jealous. I'm constantly afraid she'll be
raped … For guys who've been abused, I think sex with
females is harder. There's not one guy who's prepared to be
abused, to cope with that, to survive it. You have to learn
everything over again.

I don't trust men at all, especially those who've got a big
belly like my father has, the ones who are policemen, security
guards, or in the army like he was. I'm always at the ready, distrustful, around older men. I have a friend whose father is also
an army type and this friend has a history like mine. It makes
me wonder how many of us there are, like that. Perhaps there's
a connection because of the fact that soldiers, during a war,
they can rape women and children. In the army cadets, where
my father had enrolled me, I was afraid of being abused. I fixed

a padlock to a belt placed between my underclothes and my pants during the times I was at cadet camp. I felt it was like a chastity belt.

Last year, I made a friend, a guy in his thirties. He invited me to have a drink at his place. He was an alcoholic, a man who could be somewhat violent with his children when he was drunk. I thought I could help him. I spent a lot of time at his place during my outings from the group home. Once, when I was helping him do the dishes, he slipped a pencil between my legs, from behind. I found it rather odd, what he did. He started up again but then he went a bit too far. I turned around and hit him. He asked me what got into me. I told him my father had sexually abused me. Even so, after that he started up again, really getting on my nerves. I spoke to the people I knew about it. I thought about it all and realized he was behaving like an abuser, someone who was trying to surprise me when I wasn't expecting it. It was difficult to get him out of my life. He chased after me. But it's finished. I feel he betrayed me.

Today I have a mohawk haircut to keep people away from me. People are afraid. Another thing, my father hated that haircut. But I don't talk to my father any more. He doesn't want to speak to me. As for my mother and me, we talk a bit, but not about the abuse. She takes my father's side. She doesn't want her marriage to break up. She can't face the truth. My father's an okay guy in her eyes and that's how most people see him. He's not able to admit to himself what he did. If he were to admit it to me, or even just to himself, I'd be ready to forgive him. I still don't know why we did it. I really don't know, but I suspect he'd been abused himself as a boy.

As for me, I want to get over all this. I have serious goals in life: I want to have a good job, a family. I know I'll have to make it on my own though, without a family behind me to help. It's hard today to have to go it alone. You don't know where to start. It scares me, but at the same time it's a challenge. My girlfriend is there to back me up. I'll need it.

CHAPTER SIX

"Why Me?": Identity Confusion

Having reviewed the contradictory emotions and feelings of boys who have been victims of sexual abuse, it remains to be seen how such experiences weigh upon their identity. As we can see from the respondent interviews an impression of dispossession of the self is characteristic of men who have been sexually abused by other men. How does this impinge upon their self-image? How do they build a masculine identity? What existential questions confront them? In order to better understand the dynamics pertaining to male victims of sexual abuse in childhood, it is of prime importance to look into these elements. This chapter will deal more precisely with the identity confusion present in young men who have been so victimized. We will take an in-depth look at the discord between what they are and what they would like to be from four different viewpoints: personal identity (Who am I?), sexual identity (Am I a real man?), sexual orientation (Am I homosexual or heterosexual?), and homophobia.

"WHO AM I?"
THE QUESTION OF PERSONAL IDENTITY

Personal identity extends beyond and encompasses sexual identity. Before knowing whether one is male or female, the human being must become aware that he or she exists. According to Alex Mucchielli, identity is an internal awareness and a grouping of criteria that define the self according to one's life history and one's evolution.[1] Personal identity derives from interactions and is continually acquired and used in contact with others during real-life experience. Our understanding of the world and the place we occupy in it is what shapes our personal identity. This identity, built on individual, social, and cultural experience, in turn structures our relationship with ourselves and with others. According to sociologist Helen Rose Fuchs Ebaugh, personal identity may be destroyed and reconstructed in the wake of experiences that leave indelible impressions.[2] This is precisely what happens with boy victims of sexual abuse.

An individual can only be in harmony with himself if the elements that make up his sense of identity have been allowed to develop. Looking at the testimonies gathered in this book, most such elements are lacking in boy victims of sexual abuse. The invasion of his intimacy and the violation of his physical integrity make it difficult for the boy to acquire a positive body awareness. As we have seen, some boys experience a dichotomy between themselves and their body, as if they consisted of two separate entities. Furthermore, their isolation, loneliness, and rejection by family members creates in many of these boys the impression that they do not belong to the male community. Finally, the aggressors's imposition of his own rules and desires blocks the young male's development of a sence of autonomy, including that needed to free himself from the control imposed upon him by the observor.

A positive sense of self-esteem and even a minimal trust in others are also frequently lacking in these young men. The reference points normally provided by family or a group with shared loyalties are cruelly lacking in male victims of sexual abuse. We can understand why they say they are ill at ease with themselves, disoriented about the present and future, and without safe markers to guide them. One of the respondents states: "I am something 'other,' someone I don't really know but also someone that another person has sufficiently imagined in order to abuse him. As for me, I'm still trying to find myself." In short, these boys have only the slightest impression of "being someone," so diffuse is their identity.

Victims of incest committed by a father or brother seem to have an even more diffuse, vague, and problematic identity. "My father saw me as an object. I belonged to him. I was his thing," said one young person, explaining the difficulty he has had seeing himself as a distinct person and clarifying, at least to some extent, his relationship with his father. "Who was he, for me? My lover, my enemy, my father? And me, who was I, what was I in all of that?" When the aggressor is part of the child's daily experience, and especially if he invades the child's room or his bed, the child's most intimate space is violated in the extreme. As noted earlier, some respondents have gone so far as to describe a sense that they were taking leave of their bodies at the moment the aggression was taking place. It goes without saying that such a negation of the body and of what it experiences contributes to the breaking down of the child's identity. Who is he? What is he doing? Does this body belong to him? He prefers not to know. He is no longer really present inside it.

When a child is forced at an early age to respond to the sexual needs of others, the development of his personal identity is compromised. At the time in their childhood when most of the respondents were assaulted (around eight years old, on average) they were not ready, either physically or psychologically, to deal with the invasive sexuality imposed upon them. "You're not treated as a person, you're just a sexual object," said one of them. At a stage when the child is beginning to open up towards the outside world and to develop his own interests, abused boys see their horizon restricted to the world of sex. (Some among them will later become sexually compulsive.) Traumatized by the abuse, it becomes a source of constant preoccupation: how to escape? how to extricate himself from it? From the time the sexual abuse begins, the boy's whole life is at risk of being centred around the invading trauma, this secret, or, as it is sometimes seen, this enslavement. The child is no longer available to complete the tasks that usually await him at this time in the formation of his identity, so taken up is he by the impact of abuse (for which, in many cases, no assistance will be forthcoming).

A child's being reduced to the rank of sexual object to be used by an adolescent or an adult will ultimately introduce a doubt into his mind: could it be, perhaps, that this alone is what he is for? In this way he may also learn to concentrate on the sexual needs and desires of others to the exclusion of his own. Taken to the extreme, he will lose the ability to define his own sexuality and his own personality. He only exists through and for others. He may also start to believe that he has no identity of his own.

"AM I A REAL MAN?"
THE QUESTION OF SEXUAL IDENTITY

In the following lines, I will use the expression "sexual identity" to mean the conviction in an individual that he or she possesses the physical, psychological, or commonly assumed attributes of a male or female. The notion of sexual identity corresponds here to what some American authors call "gender identity"[3] and what certain French-language authors prefer to term "psychological sexing identity."[4] This subjective identity includes the feeling of belonging to one of the two sexes and, in a more concrete sense, the feeling of having adopted the attitudes and the behaviours socially ascribed as masculine or feminine. As Erikson has described, the acquisition of a psychological and social identity is an extremely complex process that is made up simultaneously of one relationship of belonging and another relationship of exclusion.[5] That is to say, the self is defined by its resemblances to and its differences from others. Sexual identity differs from sexual orientation, which is determined according to one's attraction towards one or the other sex, although such orientation may make up part of the individual's identity or, more exactly, serve the individual as a source of self-definition.

It is striking to observe the extent to which most of the boy victims of sexual abuse are convinced that, in terms of their sexual identity, something inside them is defective or abnormal. They believe that their aggressors must surely have noticed this abnormality, and that it is something any shrewd person will eventually discern. Although on the face of it these young men seem no different from anyone else, on the inside they are apt to feel vulnerable and insecure regarding their masculinity. This insecurity is often a central preoccupation.

Nearly all the respondents confided at one time or another during our conversations that the first questions they asked themselves were Why? Why me? Obviously, there is no response to this existential questioning, though it reveals great acuity since boys are not supposed to be violated – the victims of violation are supposed to be exclusively girls or women, at least according to popular belief. It is unthinkable that such a thing might happen to a boy, unless boys who are violated have some peculiar characteristic, something shameful that is written on their face or their body, or given away by their attitudes or behaviour. That, at least, is what abused boys come to think. And the aggressor has seen it. It is as if, in their appearance or in their identity, something has betrayed not only their vulnerability but their fundamental difference compared to other boys, compared to those boys who are never sexually molested.

This tenacious impression is bolstered by a point of view that is as much psychological as it is sociological. Nicolas Groth, in concluding his research into the masculine experience of sexual abuse, affirmed that the violation of a male is often seen, by aggressor and victim alike, as a symbolic defeat and emasculation of the victim: for the aggressor, it is an affirmation of his anger, his power, and his masculinity.[6] The feeling of possessing an inept masculinity will, in many cases, provoke inappropriate efforts by the victim to improve matters. Such efforts may range from sexual aggression to a delinquent expression of homophobia, to the compulsive pursuit of sexual relationships or to an obsession with body building and physical strength.

For some abused boys, acquiring a virile appearance and behaviour does become an obsession. While desperately seeking a response to the question "Why me?" the boy may conclude he has been chosen because of his physical appearance, because of his attitudes, his voice, the way he is dressed, or because of any other characteristic he may possess that is at all feminine or androgynous because it is believed that aggressors don't go for "real men." He will usually try to rid himself of these traits or distance himself from them. If the boy blames himself for having attracted his abuser, if he feels guilty for not having defended himself or not having put up a good enough fight, or, again, for having taken a *laissez-faire* attitude towards being sexually violated (a passivity that is culturally associated with being female or homosexual), he will try all the harder to wipe out or to compensate for his supposed lack of masculinity.

In this way, being sexually abused changes the way a young male sees himself. In our culture, does not the mere fact that he has been abused bring into consideration the three criteria of "real" manhood? As I mentioned at the very beginning of this work, conformity with the virile masculine model requires that a boy convince himself and others that he is not a child (not dependent or vulnerable), not a woman (without passivity and not compliant sexually), and not homosexual (not sexually attracted to other men). All boys abused by other males must measure themselves against these three requirements. No wonder then that they have reason to ask themselves questions, nourish uncertainties, and entertain anxiety.

Some victims become sexual aggressors themselves to prove that they too are virile – something they see as synonymous with being dominating. To become abusive could be a way to conspire against one's fate as a victim. Some respondents, having themselves committed abuse, affirm that for them it was a way to understand "from the inside" their aggressor's motivations. However, while identifying with the abuser enables some abused boys to strengthen their tenuous sense of masculinity, it is neither a universal nor an automatic response to being abused. Yet this transitition from the role of victim to that of abuser can bring a symbolic resolution to some of their identity confusion, since "real men" are never among those who are dominated. Thus, it is much easier for boys than for girls to identify in the end with their aggressors, particularly when the boy victim seeks to strengthen his own masculine self-image.

Florence Rush has noted that boys who feel diminished and feminized by an abusive experience will feel more humiliated than those who come to identify with the abuser, or who themselves become abusive, since the latter lose less of their self-esteem. (For a boy or man, what is important is to protect or to regain his virility, his superiority, his dominance.) The author explains:

Gender is a flexible term. Masculine or feminine does not necessarily correspond to those who are male and female. Women and male and female children are often patiently, indulgently, condescendingly or angrily seen as weak, dependent and helpless. Gender difference, unlike sexual difference, implies masculine superiority and feminine inferiority, and since the prototype of romantic or sexual love contains the formula of one dominant and one subordinate partner, men sometimes select a person of the same sex but opposite gender as a sex partner. A man in prison will, without injuiry to his masculinity, rape another inmate who is young, thin, fair and vulnerable enough to be taken for "feminine"; a soldier will sometimes rape not only women and children, but also conquered men to assert himself as conqueror.[7]

Rush postulated that men who abuse male children would be more heterosexual than homosexual, since it is "femininity" or vulnerability coupled with the immaturity of the boy that excites them. In his work on rape, Daniel Welzer-Lang confirms this assertion, underlining that there is no intrinsic relationship between gender and biological sex.[8] A male child sexually used by an adult male may very well be seen by the adult as being of feminine gender. Rapes committed in prisons illustrate a parallel situation: while the rapist is not seen as a homosexual, his victim, younger and weaker, will be labelled as such. Since the vast majority of my respondents reported that they had been abused by men who describe themselves as heterosexual, it is not surprising that they worry about their masculinity. They have attracted men who were not normally attracted by men.

As psychoanalyst Robert Stoller has noted, the sense of sexual identity or gender involves two things: the awareness that "I am a man," and the belief that "I am strong."[9] Abused boys feel they have failed on both counts. Having allowed another male to abuse them, something a "real man" would not have allowed, they are not men. They are not strong or virile in their own eyes as long as they have not proven or symbolically re-established their masculinity. One preferred way of achieving this and affirming one's virility is by accumulating sexual adventures with women. The testimonies of some of the young people I interviewed are eloquent in this regard, revealing that the principal aim of their numerous sexual conquests is indeed not pleasure – some of them find little pleasure therein. Rather it is to prove that girls find them attractive and that the young men are able to provide the girls with sexual pleasure. In this case one can probably speak of compulsive heterosexuality, a heterosexuality that responds less to the in-depth needs of the individual than to his fear of being homosexual. Misdemeanours such as theft and physical aggression, carried out with a view to reversing the young man's view of himself as powerless and victimized, also serve the need to prove his virility. Doubtless male victims are susceptible to the impulse to direct their rage against others through aggressive or antisocial conduct since such behaviour can relate to a need to affirm a certain virility.

HOMO OR HETERO?
THE QUESTION OF SEXUAL ORIENTATION

During the interviews, the bewilderment of the respondents over their sexual orientation often constituted one of the strong points of the interview, so numerous and so fraught with anxiety were their preoccupations regarding this topic. "If I've had homosexual relations, does that mean I am a homosexual? If I've had physical reactions – erection or ejaculation – is that a sign that I liked it? If I don't like it when my girl-friend touches me or takes the initiative in love-making, does it mean that I don't like women?" Ex-victims of sexual abuse are plagued by such questions.

Two out of three participants in this study revealed that they had had fantasies of a homosexual nature, no matter what their declared sexual orientation. This finding, surprising as it may seem, is nonetheless in agreement with the statistics available on the subject. The American researcher David Finkelhor has no hesitation in affirming that boys abused before the age of thirteen are four times more likely than others to relive homosexual experiences.[10] What he is not explicit about, however, is what type of homosexual relations this refers to. The present research shows that such relations are at great risk of being poorly integrated, as far as our respondents who have indeed had homosexual relations have indicated. In many cases, homosexuality is experienced within a climate of guilt, rejection of the other, or denial of one's own needs, when it is not undertaken in a compulsive mode that cancels out any real satisfaction. Similar reactions may of course be engendered or increased by the social stigmatizing of homosexuality. Without doubt, however, the homosexual nature of their abuse often gives rise to a confusion between sexual submission and homosexuality in the minds of ex-victims. Thus, three of the respondents who had homosexual relations with men quite a bit older than themselves, involving considerations for services rendered, have a hard time imagining that it could be otherwise, as though inequality were an inevitable condition of every (homo)sexual relationship.

Psychologists Johnson and Shrier[11] state that many more boys who were abused by men will later describe themselves as homosexual or bisexual (six to seven times more on average) than boys who were abused by women. But should we not ask whether this is necessarily a cause-and-effect situation or whether there is simply a correlation? Could a homosexual or bisexual orientation result from sexual abuse? Is it independent of it? Would boys who already show a certain homosexual tendency be more susceptible to being abused as "punishment" for their non-conformity to the masculine stereotype? Anthropologist Daniel Welzer-Lang[12] suggests this last possibility be explored – not without reason.

Susan Wachob,[13] an American therapist, has pointed out that boys who are "pre-homosexual" are earmarked for sexual abuse. Such boys would not necessarily be chosen because they were suspected of being gay but because they were more isolated and therefore more desirous of attention or acceptance than others because of their burgeoning "difference." Our culture integrates with difficulty young boys who are considered as atypical, especially when they distance themselves from their assigned roles or from the behaviours expected of them because of their sex or gender. Wachob also states that boys who are non-conformists are very rapidly categorized as effeminate. She even believes that abuse may be the direct or indirect effect of the hatred of fathers or relatives who are heterosexual and homophobic and who sense that this child is different: abuse will serve to warn him or provide a "well merited" punishment. Besides, young "pre-homosexuals" would supposedly be more susceptible not only to keeping the secret to which they are already becoming habituated concerning their sexual orientation but also to repressing their real feelings and needs. Information gathered for this study in part supports such hypotheses: at least five respondents believe that their father or brother took advantage of their homosexual curiosity in abusing them. Without identifying themselves as homosexual or bisexual, other boys believe that an androgynous part of their personality make-up attracted the aggressor.

On the other hand, several respondents believe that their homosexual tendencies result from their abuse. The psychoanalyst Robert Stoller confirms that a brief homosexual apprenticeship could be fundamental in determining sexual orientation if it takes place at a critical stage of development.[14] This is not to say that a homosexual-type rape necessarily engenders a homosexual orientation in the victim. There is no automatic connection between the experience of sexual abuse by a young male and his subsequent homosexuality. Sexual victimization does not cause homosexuality: this is proven by the fact that the majority of homosexual men have not been sexually abused in childhood or adolescence. However, and this nuance is important, the sensations experienced during an act of sexual aggression may leave a lasting impression that amounts to a kind of conditioning. The American author William

Prendergast goes so far as to speak of a sexual imprinting, which at one time will be expressed positively and at another negatively.[15] That is to say, sexual abuse of a homosexual nature may just as easily incite a boy to repeat certain acts that he has tried and subsequently eroticized as it may keep him away from such acts in the future because he experienced an insuperable revulsion to them. These are not the only ways of reacting to abuse, of course. The experience may also engender some ambivalence. What is significant is that in many cases the individual is confused about his sexual orientation. This would explain, partially at least, why some boys will end up as nude dancers or prostitutes in a homosexual environment while describing themselves neither as homosexual nor as bisexual but as homophobic.

Concerning the prevalence of sexual abuse in men whose orientation is homosexual or bisexual, a recent statistic proves particularly interesting. It shows that Stoller, Finkelhor, Johnson, and Shrier are not wrong in emphasizing that the percentage of sexually abused boys who later manifest a homosexual interest is higher than that among the non-abused population. According to an article that analyses the first twenty-five hundred replies to a scientific research questionnaire for readers, published in a gay magazine, the *Advocate*, twenty-one percent of respondents consider themselves to have been victims of sexual abuse before the age of sixteen.[16] This proportion is higher than that found in the masculine population in general. Even if it does not signify that suffering sexual abuse leads to a homosexual or bisexual orientation, two or three hypotheses nevertheless merit serious consideration: that children who are atypical as to their gender identity or their burgeoning sexual orientation are more likely to be the target of sexual aggression; that experiences undergone during sexual victimization tend to mould the sexual behaviour of victims through a learning process (be it unconscious and involuntary); and finally, that undergoing sexual abuse may in some cases by seen as a revelation of homosexuality, even if the men reporting on the matter are unanimous in saying they would have liked to be "initiated" some other way.[17]

If being homosexual is for some ex-victims of sexual abuse difficult to endure, the situation is hardly easier for those of heterosexual preference or orientation. The testimonies of numerous boys in my study underline the importance of their first heterosexual relations in confirming their normality. The success of their very first heterosexual encounter brings great relief, like a victory:

they have been able to prove to themselves and to demonstrate to others that they can have relations with the opposite sex. For many of these men, the only acceptable object of desire is a woman; hence they wish to be desired by women only. Unfortunately, their relationships with women are often problematic, judging by the remarks of respondents on their former or present heterosexual relationships. Many speak of a high degree of emotional instability, of a love life that hovers between total abstinence and sexual promiscuity. Sometimes an excessive or compulsive heterosexuality is apparent whereby their desire for sexual contact can never be satiated. In their sexual confusion they resemble the homosexual respondents in my research.

Some respondents had put off their first sexual relationship with a girl, afraid that it would be obvious they had been abused by a man and that a girl might then consider them abnormal. These respondents worried they would not behave like other boys their own age, or that others might see that there was something vulnerable, effeminate, not manly about them. Even once the uneasiness had been overcome, their sexual relations were not always as satisfying as they had anticipated. For example, many said that they were haunted by memories of the abuse and thus had difficulty in enjoying the sexual pleasure they felt; others described themselves as indifferent towards their own enjoyment, even pushing away the partner who was trying to pleasure them, all of which only served to nourish the dilemma as to their real sexual preference.

In our society, sexuality is seen as a means of self-discovery, as if sensual pleasure reveals to us, even arouses in us, our most secret feelings and our most intimate needs. The relationships and sexual feelings experienced within an abusive situation, above all if they are the very first the victim has experienced (which is often the case), will have conjured up certain complementary sexual images of self and other – dominating-dominated, passive-active, male-female – which an abuse victim may erroneously presume to be indicative of his innermost propensities. Here in lies an abused boy's potential confusion in determining the "true nature" of his sexuality.

The stronger the boy's impression that he has participated actively in the sexual relations initiated by his aggressor, the stronger his sense that he has revealed himself to be "feminine" or "homosexual" and the more he will internalize the burden of this revelation. If the boy has acknowledged to himself that he felt physical gratification while being abused by another male, the chances that he will describe himself as homosexual or bisexual are obviously even greater. The abuse will seem to him all the more like an initiation. He will discern in his physical receptivity a sign of his true nature. He is unaware that a child or an adolescent can respond to a vast spectrum of genital stimulation, even if such stimulation is absent from his own fantasies – if he already has fantasies – or his own expectations.

Several respondents reported having occasional homosexual relations while living with a heterosexual partner, without defining themselves as homosexual or bisexual. The tendency to dissociate sexual behaviour from sexual orientation is common among such respondents. "I do things of a homosexual nature but I am not homosexual," some of these men will tell themselves. Their reasoning is not necessarily erroneous, since homosexual behaviour is in no way synonymous with or predictive of a permanent or exclusive homosexual preference. Conversely, it is also true that if some of a victim's behaviour should be labelled as homosexual, the young man may be encouraged to believe himself homosexual or bisexual and to act accordingly, even if his fantasies and his everyday or initial sexual settings were heterosexual in nature.

The established opposition in our culture between homosexuality and heterosexuality leads to the illogical idea that one lone homosexual episode could signal an innate homosexuality. This "essentialist"[18] view of homosexuality as a source of identity, a vision to which numerous respondents adhere, incites them to see themselves as torn between two identities. "Am I heterosexual or homosexual?" In many cases, the homosexual dimension of the abuse will quite simply be denied in order to escape the dilemma. One boy reported that his parents reacted more to the homosexual nature of the abuse than to its actual after-effects. "If the adult had been a woman, I don't think they would have done anything. When it comes down to it, they were afraid I would become homosexual." This leads us to look at the question of homophobia among abused boys – and in our society overall.

AN IRRATIONAL FEAR:
THE HOMOPHOBIA QUESTION

The silence of boys who have been victims of sexual abuse is partially explained by their fear of being taken for homosexuals.

Moreover, their desire to prove they have nothing at all to do with homosexuality can lead not only to a prodigal heterosexuality but also to an almost obsessive homophobia.

Paradoxically, words and practices that are plainly homophobic are juxtaposed by some victims with free engagement in homosexual activities. Francis is a case in point. He was going into Montreal's gay village to beat up men he believed to be homosexual while he himself was having fantasies around, and homosexual relations with one of his gay-bashing buddies. Both of them were able to convince themselves that they were not homosexual on the grounds that they were beating up on gays. These adolescents could have intimate homosexual relations quite calmly "between real men." Although their manifestations are not necessarily so extreme, diverse degrees of ambivalence can be discerned in several respondents: they hate homosexuals while at the same time entertaining fantasies or even relations that are homosexual.

Mistakenly to see a correlation between sexual abuse and homosexuality can easily generate a vengeful homophobia in those who have concluded that all homosexual men are potential abusers. As psychiatrist Michael Myers has emphasized, ambiguity about their sexual orientation, together with a certain homophobia, is very common in sexually abused boys.[19] One researcher in this field, John Sebold, has gone so far as to say that the most conclusive indicator of sexual abuse in boys is precisely their homophobic preoccupations.[20] These manifest themselves in different ways, such as constant reference to the presumed or known homosexual orientation of other boys; a strong need to convince their peers of their heterosexuality; constant talk about women and their sexual exploits, real or imaginary, with them; intolerance regarding the effeminacy of others; dissociation from anything that might be perceived as homosexual in inclination; revulsion concerning masturbation, which is seen as a homosexual act; and manifestation of nervousness when grappling with the homosexual nature of the abuse.

Vacillating at times between wanting to repeat certain aspects of the abuse (especially aspects that were to some extent gratifying) and then at other times having a keen aversion to them, some young victims become decidedly homophobic. They will take on an aggressive way of talking or behaving around gays or bisexuals, whom they automatically consider to be potential abusers. Let us remember, however, that the abusers of these boys generally identified themselves as heterosexual and in some cases used homophobic language themselves. Even in ex-victims who say their orientation is homosexual, the picture they have of homosexuality is hardly positive; witness the remarks of a young respondent who says he is gay: "One should not allow homosexuals to bring up children. It isn't normal. It would give the children a bad example. Homosexuality is the worst thing that can happen to you." This kind of attitude is termed internalized homophobia.

It is clear that, for the majority of the respondents, the homosexual nature of the abuse raises the question of their own homosexual tendencies whether or not they actualize such potential. The idea that if you do not detest homosexuals you must be "one of them" seems obvious to many ex-victims, especially the youngest. They seem to say to themselves that, if they do not clearly demonstrate that they are homophobic, everyone will believe they liked having sexual relations with the person who abused them. Some will admit that they knowingly act like a redneck for fear of being considered homosexual, although the requisite machismo does not really correspond to their inner feelings: "I give the impression I'm a rocker, but I'm not that type. It's just to get respect, to avoid anyone getting close to me. Deep down, I'm supersensitive. But I have no choice. I have to protect myself."

One adolescent who was abused by his cousin admits he felt reassured when, for the first time, he watched some pornographic films his father had brought home. He realized he was capable of heterosexual responses and this reduced his fear of becoming homosexual: "I couldn't care less about the ones who call me homo because I was abused. It doesn't get to me, because I know I'm interested in women. Before, yes it's true, I was afraid of doing the same thing. Today, homos, I can sniff them out. If one of them tries it on with me, I'll punch him in the face. Once, I discovered I was in the gay village. When I saw two fellows holding hands, I took off like a shot."

Another young respondent confides: "I lose control if a man touches me ... If a fag touched me, grabbed my butt for example, he'd get my fist in his face." A third, and this is more rare, is conscious that it's his own homosexuality that frightens him: "When I'm outside and see a good-looking guy I'm attracted to, I have to cross to the other side of the street. I'm all too aware of my feelings."

The confusion between homosexual identity and homosexual attraction is certainly not the prerogative of male victims of sexual abuse, but it is heavily represented in their language: to be heterosexual is to be masculine; to be homosexual is to be feminine, or at least to be effeminate and submissive. For some of the respondents, being masculine is the opposite of being vulnerable or being victimized as they have been. Hence the boasting about their (hetero)sexual achievements or their physical prowess (roughness with others, toughness in respect to their own body, obsession with physical development and physical performance). In short, they are once more "real men" and they want the whole world to know it.

Nevertheless, in their ambivalence, some of these former victims seem to be "playing with fire": they are at the same time attracted to and disgusted by homosexuality. Amid great anxiety, albeit mixed with a definite curiosity, some of the boys come to entertain homosexual and homophobic preoccupations simultaneously. Bruno's case speaks eloquently to this subject. He says he detests homosexuals but that, when he is out walking at night, he hesitates between two possibilities; he could chase them or he could invite them to make love with him. His recent experiences demonstrate that he is indeed quite capable of adopting either attitude successfully. What is more, some young fellows are afraid of being victimized again but they willingly put themselves in potential risk situations: they frequent a milieu known for homosexual prostitution; they have exhibitionist tendencies (dancing nude or posing for erotic photographs intended for a homosexual clientele), or they visit places known to be frequented by homosexual men. Assuredly they are attempting to exorcise past traumatisms. But at what price? Some indeed find themselves in situations that remind them of their initial abuse. Such situations merely reinforce their fear that any man might be interested in them sexually and abuse them.

Overt and growing homophobia can evolve into violence. For certain male victims, to assault someone else, in particular a homosexual who is imagined to be in the same category as the abuser, will exorcise his fear. Some respondents have envisaged this possibility and at least one has realized it. He and his buddies (among whom there is at least one other ex-victim) proved to themselves that they were the strongest, that they had conquered the monster, that they had regained their masculinity by coming to blows with those who, in their eyes, symbolically represented all abusers. The fear of the homosexual, traditionally and wrongly associated with the paedophile, and the disparagement of the homosexuality felt to be either present or latent within themselves often creates, in men who have been sexually abused in childhood, a strong malaise that must not be underestimated. Perhaps sociologist Christophe Gentaz is correct when he writes that homophobia acts like a psychological condom on their manhood.[21]

Conversely, associating in friendship with gay or bisexual men is perhaps, for some, a way to rid themselves of their traumas. It could demonstrate that they are able to entertain a relationship with a man who is attracted to other men, and potentially to them, while maintaining mastery of the situation, or at least having the impression of so doing. It gives them some comfort to tell themselves that from now on they are the smartest: they have taken back power over themselves and over those they distrust. This reaction suggests that, sometimes, that for which one feels the most repugnance is also that to which one is most attracted. Conquering one's fear demands that the individual test it, up to a certain point. It has been said by Freudians and behaviourists alike that to get close to the source of one's anxiety is the preferred method of overcoming it. The paradox is only too obvious: homophobia does not necessarily preclude becoming acquainted with homosexual men or frequenting a homosexual milieu and both behaviours are often present in men who have been sexually abused by other men.

BRUNO'S STORY

Bruno, twenty-five years old, was sexually abused by his father from the time he was six years old until he was fourteen.

My father was, in fact, my stepfather, and I never knew my real father. He left when I was a baby. My mother already had two other children, also boys.

I was six years old when it first happened. I didn't know anything about sex. I just used to do what he asked me. He was my father, so I did what he said. I knew it was a secret because he asked me not to talk about it, but I thought it was okay. Well, more or less. And he was doing the same thing with my brothers. When I realized a few years later that it wasn't normal, I told my mother about it. She said she'd see to it. But she didn't do anything. At least, she didn't change her behaviour towards him. Even today, I'm still mad at my mother. She died later on.

When you're obliged to do that, you might just as well get some pleasure out of it. In any case, you can't prevent your body feeling things. When I was nine or ten, I started to refuse him, mostly because he was trying to force me to have sex with my brothers in front of him. At that time, too, he was paying one of my cousins who was fourteen to have sex with him. One day he wanted me to take part in a threesome with that cousin. At least it wasn't as bad as making love with one of my own brothers. From then on, my cousin started making me drink when my father wasn't there. The first time I got loaded was with that fourteen-year-old cousin, when I was nine or ten. He had asked me if I liked to drink. I had replied that my father wouldn't allow me to because I was far too young. He went out and bought a large case of beer. I drank half of it, and then we got sexual. I thought my cousin had a great body. He was young, like me. Today, I don't see what he did as abusive, even though I don't think I'd have gone along with it so easily if he hadn't made me drink the beer. I'm not a homo. I ask myself whether my habit of drinking before making love doesn't stem from that. I've never made love sober since then. My father didn't hesitate to take advantage of it when he found out I liked to drink. By nine o'clock on Saturday mornings we were

drinking together. By ten or eleven o'clock I was drunk. You
can guess the rest.

My father used to say I had a huge penis. He liked to
sodomize me too. At first it used to hurt, but somehow I got to
like it later on. To begin with he would buy me off with small
favours, like twenty-five cents or candy. After, he had to
increase the amount he was paying me or he'd threaten me:
he'd say he would ground me, refuse to pay for my spare-time
activities, things like that.

Girls? I didn't discover them until my adolescence. All the
guys were saying how fantastic it was to go with a girl. But I'd
only ever been with guys. I was keen to see how it was with a
girl and I got the opportunity when I spent a weekend with a
girl cousin. I was fourteen. She was about ten years older. She
came into my room in the morning to help me make my bed.
I had a feeling something was going to happen. The thought
was already forming in my head. We must both have been
thinking about it. We started roughing each other up, then
somehow we fell on the bed and it just happened, all by itself –
we made love. Even if she was my cousin and even if she was
older than me, I didn't see it as abuse. On the contrary, I told
myself she had introduced me to something a bit more normal.
From then on I was able to continue with girls, quite normally.

Sometimes I regret not wanting to denounce my father. My
girl cousin, the first person I spoke to about it, suggested I do
it. When my father realized he was getting into hot water, he
said he would get help, promised he'd do all he could ... It all
stopped when I started living on my own. I was fifteen years
old. That's how it all stopped, or almost, because he didn't give
up easily, my father. He used to come and visit me in my apartment and he was still trying it on. At one point we were living
quite close to one another. We had each other's keys in case of
emergencies. One night, I heard a noise. He was tip-toeing in.
He was in my room, looking at me. I had the impression he
was masturbating. I leapt out of bed and yelled: "What do you
think you're doing?" He mumbled something or other. I threw
him out. That's one of the last times we saw each other. He
must have realized I was at the end of my rope with him. He
was probably afraid I would speak out or that I'd denounce
him, because, you know, I was really pissed off with him.

Abuse like I went through, it's like a time bomb in your head. You never know when it'll go off. And from the beginning I've had all sorts of problems as a result of it. At school I didn't do well. I couldn't concentrate. It was better for me to get a job as soon as I could. I've never been out of a job since. I'm quite a serious worker, but then I've had to look after myself all alone.

My main problem today is that I think about sex all the time. I'm obsessed with it from morning till night. Women, men, sex is all I think about. For sure, I prefer women, but it's much easier with men. With women, you have to put white gloves on, you have to take the time to persuade them. Even when it's your sweetheart, she's not willing all the time. And then again, they get serious right away. It's not easy just to have a bit of fun with a girl. Men, they're always ready for sex, and afterwards it's like "Don't know him, never seen him." If I went about it the same way with a girl as I do with men, she'd think I was a sex maniac. My favourite trick is to wait in the park or in a public toilet until a man comes in. Then, if he hangs around, if he's looking at me ... there are lots of ways to tell if he's interested ... and since I'm quite good looking ...

Before getting serious with a girl like I am right now, I had all sorts of adventures with women too: colleagues from work, their friends, girls I met in bars and discos ... We'd often end up in bed. I made it a point of honour to get laid by all of them. But it would lead to bickering because girls are often jealous of one another. That's one of the reasons why I'm less active in that department than I was before. I'm less attracted to men, but for me it's more practical.

In the summer what I do is I take a walk in the park. I know the best places. I stretch out on the grass, away from the crowd. I take off my shirt. I like to be looked at and admired. It's strange: in my head I find the thought of two men together disgusting, but when I get aroused, I can't resist any temptation, homo or hetero. If a male approaches and he looks good to me, then I let him get on with it. If I don't like the look of him and he's getting too close, then I say: "Hey, what are you up to? Leave me alone, you damned fag!" I can look nasty when I want. The guy takes off soon enough.

What excites me most is a sense of danger. I get a thrill out of it. Actually, men probably excite me less than the context in

which things are happening. Getting it on with a guy, undis-
turbed, in a bedroom, with a little background music playing,
that's okay for homosexuals. But that doesn't interest me. What
I want is the risk, the fear of being found out, being surprised.

With my girlfriend, if I don't take the initiative, we don't get
into it. I don't like a girl to make the first move. We don't seem
to be too well synchronized, her and me. When I want it, she's
tired. When she feels like it, I'm the one who doesn't want it.
With her, it's more about affection and understanding. That
holds me. And then, her folks adore me, which makes me feel
I belong in a family, at last. I feel loved for my own self for the
first time in my life. This is very important for me and it's why
I'll stay with her as long as she wants me.

When I was a little younger, I knew some men who were
quite wealthy. No, I wasn't prostituting. Let's just say I was
indulging myself. I did get something out of it, but when it
came to a choice between that kind of life and women, I didn't
hesitate. With a man, I would always have felt ill at ease. It's
not really the way I want to live. The light went on one time
when I was out with a man. He wanted to buy me a Walkman
and the salesgirl said: "That's nice. Daddy's paying, eh?" I felt
really awkward. He was about the same age as my father. My
whole past went through my mind in just a few seconds and
I told myself no way was my future going to look like that.
I split. At the same time, I had just met the woman I'm now
living with. I made the right choice. I've never regretted it. I've
never loved anyone as much as I love that girl. I'd be mad at
myself if I made her unhappy. I don't like lying to her about
my life, but I have no choice. She wouldn't understand.

Am I homo or hetero? I see myself as a hetero. Homosexuality is not for me. I'm sure it stems from the abuse. If I hadn't
learned about that kind of sex, I don't know if I would have
thought of it all by myself. I'm only attracted to older males
now. I like to think the man also finds me attractive, so that
I can do anything I want with him.

It's like I have two personalities: the good little boy on the
one hand and the sex maniac on the other. I don't find it
normal to be thinking about sex all the time. I'm afraid it will
end up ruining my life. Suppose I were arrested, or if the girl
I love found out about it. Maybe I need some therapy but

I don't see myself going to talk about it. I've heard it said there
are groups for male victims of sexual abuse and groups for "sex
addicts" too, but I can't see myself telling the story of my life in
front of everyone.

As for my father, I get news of him indirectly through the
family. He's remarried. I hope he's not doing the same thing to
other kids. His wife can't have any. No one will ever be able to
trust him. He looks like a decent fellow, but he has no control
over himself sexually. I don't know whether he's a paedophile,
a homosexual, or whatever, but I don't think he feels right
about himself. My brothers don't want to see him any more,
either. They're older than I am. They have kids. For sure, they
don't want to risk their children becoming sexual abuse victims
like they were.

PAUL'S STORY

Paul, twenty-eight, was first sexually abused by his father, then by his brothers, and then by strangers.

I was abused from the time I was five years old by members of my family. It wasn't very long ago that it all stopped, when I was twenty-four years old. My first memories go back to when I was about three. I was put in different foster homes because my mother had psychological problems and she already had a large family to look after. I can still see it in my mind: I can see the lady who looked after me in the foster home putting me in a bath full of ice when I wet my pants or when I was a nuisance. My mother came to get me sometimes, but it wasn't often and I never stayed with her very long. I always went back to a foster home. In spite of being badly treated, I liked it better in the foster home than I did at home: there was too much yelling and fighting at home.

I was often in tears because of the fights at home. My mother used to say that boys don't cry. To punish me she would stand me in front of the mirror, while she humiliated me in front of my brothers and sisters. She would say: "Look at that cry baby, see how you look! You're not even a man, you're nothing but a scaredy cat ..." There was no tenderness or love in our house. Not for me anyway. My mother was sounding off all the time. I never could do anything right as far as she was concerned.

There were ten of us and I was the youngest. My older brothers and sisters were more pampered than I was. I wasn't allowed to eat at the table with the others, my mother said, because there were too many of us. I was happy to get the leftovers which she brought me in the living-room. My mother never took me in her arms. My father even less. He was one of those men who don't know how to pick up a child, even later when he had grandchildren. He just didn't care to see them. He said they got on his nerves. With us, his children, he was always in a bad mood. He too must certainly have had some psychological problems.

One day when we had visitors at home, I had to sleep on the sofa in the living-room and let someone else have my bed. That's when it all began. I was sleeping on my stomach, in my underwear. Half asleep, I felt someone come up behind me, pull down my shorts, and penetrate my rectum. I was so afraid that I didn't dare turn over. I could hear his heavy breathing, feel his breath, but I couldn't see him. I believe it was my father because I knew how he smelled, how big he was. I had no idea what to do, what to say. I hurt all over. I was bleeding from the rectum. The next day I stayed in bed, I couldn't stop bawling. For a long time after that, whenever I got nervous, I would mess in my pants. That's what happened to me the next day when I suddenly became scared he'd start up again. Maybe it was a physical problem because of the dilated rectum, perhaps it was psychological. I don't know, but I had that problem for years. I was doubly traumatized: first the abuse and then not being able to control my bowel movements when I was under stress.

The day I was raped I lost something and never got it back. I never feel happy; never feel that I'm normal. There's something missing: I have no purpose in life and I get no joy in living. I became rebellious with everyone. And I've stayed that way.

Soon afterwards, my brothers began abusing me too. I was about six or seven. They were adolescents. At one point, one of them took me into the woods. He was making a drawing and wanted to draw me in the nude. He sat me down on a rock, up in the mountains. We weren't far from home. I didn't know what was going on when he carressed me but somehow I was pleased to have some of his attention. At that point I didn't have any idea of what's normal and what's not normal. But he wasn't violent. I discovered my own body and his too. Later on, he started up again. He was nice with me until I refused to go further. He was asking me to lick his penis, then his rectum. I was disgusted. I tried to resist him but I had no choice.

One day when my parents weren't home, I heard one of my sisters yelling. My brother was in the bathroom with her. He was trying to penetrate her. She was ten years old. I decided to tell my mother about it, to denounce my brother. My sister, she didn't want to let on. My mother took her to see the doctor and he said she was still a virgin. They all took me for a fool, for a liar. My brother was really mad at me. To punish me, he demanded I do it more often with him, or else he would rape my sister.

A short while after all this, I noticed, during the night that
my sixteen- and seventeen-year-old brothers were quietly luring
my sisters into the bathrooms. I knew what was going on. I was
traumatized and told myself it was better I sacrifice myself to
save my sisters.

What my brothers asked me to do was disgusting. I don't
know where on earth they got such ideas. One of them uri-
nated in my face. Another time he shat on me. He was laughing, he found it amusing. I was crying and I ran away from
them. A bit later my eldest sister asked me to have sex with
her. She was laughing at me because I still didn't have erections. She said I had a small penis. I felt ill at ease. I find it
hard, being humiliated.

I ran away from home. The first time, I was eight years old.
I was walking alone along the highway. Some policemen
arrested me and locked me up at the police station because
I refused to give them my name or say where I was going, for
fear of being returned to my parents. Someone from the village
recognized me. They took me home. My father beat me. But
I did it again at the first opportunity. I felt like a prisoner,
rejected, with no one who understood me or loved me. And
then there was the shame of everything I had done. My grandfather and my godfather, the only ones who loved me, died that
year. I was very upset: there was no one else I was fond of.

When I was ten years old, I started touching the small children I used to babysit. I would undress them, touch their genitals. That was as far as it went. I knew it wasn't right but
I didn't feel okay enough to do it with children my own age.
I think I wanted to find out for myself what my brothers had
got out of it.

Around the age of eleven, I started hitch-hiking on the big
highway. I was looking for attention, for affection. Anybody
would do. Sometimes cars would stop and pick me up. I didn't
dare say no when they asked me to fellate them. First, they
would touch me, checking me out to see how I would react.
When they could see that I appeared to be okay with the idea,
that I wouldn't make a fuss, they would pull over and stop further on. They would do what had to be done in the woods or
in a field.

About that same time I began doing drugs – hash to start
with. You know, I was more or less a loner as an adolescent.

I would have liked to have had a girl interested in me, but I didn't attract girls. I must admit I wasn't comfortable too with myself. I was full of complexes, fears, and sensitivities. My brothers were making fun of me because I still wasn't ejaculating at the age of eleven. I was wondering how to go about getting involved with girls.

Towards the age of twelve, I joined the army cadets. It was supposed to make a man of me, but I still saw myself as inferior to others. The summer I turned thirteen, I went to summer camp. There I met a girl who fell in love with me. A beautiful girl, an American Indian. She let me fondle her, but I couldn't really take it any further than that. From then on I was having wet dreams. I really don't know if that's normal, either. I'm fantasizing about a slender oriental girl, with long hair, very soft and sweet as oriental women are: that's always been my fantasy. But since I'm not macho, not violent, I've never been attractive to girls.

The first time I masturbated on a child was when I was babysitting the daughter of one of my brothers. She must have been about two or three. I took off her diaper and rubbed my penis against her private parts. I didn't want to penetrate her, just to feel her next to me. I did it again a few more times before I began to be afraid of what I might do. I stopped. I realized I wasn't normal. To put it out of my mind I used to drink. I was stealing pills, taking drugs. Perhaps it was the softness of the baby that attracted me to her. Still today, with women, I never feel completely satisfied sexually. It's children who excite me the most, although I don't want to touch them any more.

As an adolescent, I began to cut myself, to carve into my arm because I was mad at myself. I was unable to express my violence except against myself. I had other problems. I had begun to masturbate more or less anywhere, openly, in the classroom, on the bus. It was like an experiment for me. I was putting objects into my rectum too. That way, I wasn't hurting anyone else. I find it difficult to accept my sexuality.

Finally, my mother took me to see a psychologist. I was put in a group home again, like I was before. I felt even more misunderstood. The educators told me my behaviour wasn't yet criminal and that it was quite possible I could get over it. In the end I started a fire in the group home. It was out of rebellion, taking revenge against the other boys who had never really accepted me. After that they put me in a detention centre for juvenile delinquents until my eighteenth birthday. They tried to get me to speak about my past but I couldn't destroy my family. In spite of everything, I stayed silent, kept it all to myself.

When I came out of the detention centre at eighteen, one of my brothers who had sexually abused me agreed to take me in. When his wife wasn't there he continued like before. We took drugs together. I was never able to say no. Rather than resist, I just felt sorry for myself. I realized that the more things change the more they stay the same.

I found myself a small job in a centre for seniors. It was with one of the employees there that I had my first complete sexual experience with a woman. I was nineteen. She started it by showing me her breasts. My brother had already pointed out to me that she was a nymphomaniac, so I thought I could get some satisfaction, go all the way with her. When all's said and done, she wasn't a bad girl. I was with her for two or three months but I discovered she was lacking in experience and that we weren't doing much in the way of sex. I realized that men knew more about how to go about it. After I lost my job because of budget cuts, we didn't see each other anymore. I was disheartened to realize that, with my particular history, I was very difficult to satisfy sexually.

The only person who really brought me pleasure was a transvestite. This was later, when I did time in prison. I was also having relations with an old guy there who loaned me money. I wasn't interested in him at all. I simply needed money for drugs. They had quickly become my big problem. I was drunk or drugged from morning to night.

In the end I stole money from my brother and went to live in town. When I had no more cash left, I found myself on the street. A homosexual picked me up and took me in. After a few days, he asked me to have sex with him. I didn't say no. Having sex had become a habit for me. I no longer even asked myself if I preferred males or females. I don't consider myself a homosexual: in my fantasy life I prefer women or children.

I began stealing to make ends meet. Stealing from clients when you're prostituting is fairly simple. I often found myself in prison. I was in, I was out, just for small offences. I tried to hang myself. I messed it up. They took away my clothes and put me in the hole. Once again, I was belittled, humiliated.

After that, I wanted to take vows, enter the Church. I was quite serious about it, but in the end I gave up the idea. I didn't know which religious group to join. I went from one to the other, did the rounds: Jehovah's Witnesses and so on. As soon as I felt welcome somewhere I started thinking about stealing from them, hurting them. I had no idea how to express any love I had for them. I'm more at home with doing wrong than I am with what is right. It suits me better in some way. Having put myself in situations where I was repeatedly called a good for nothing, a loser, I came to believe it, to live it.

I have violent thoughts about buying weapons and getting some revenge. I know there's something missing, something dead inside me that I'll never get back. I rail against this. But, you know, when I was little, I was a romantic … wrote poetry … The girls thought it was beautiful. I even wrote poetry for my friends' girlfriends. I would have turned out quite different if these things hadn't happened to me.

I've stopped seeing my brothers. That's how all the abuse ended. A year or two ago a social worker convinced me to speak to my parents about it and take my brothers to court. My mother said if I did such a thing she'd disown me. Those two brothers are well placed socially. They've continued their education, they have businesses. They're doing well and have good marriages. Just the same, I wouldn't be surprised if they sexually abuse their children. One of them was still taking a shower with his daughter when she was nine years old. I don't think a father has any business being in the shower with his daughter when she's that age. Apparently his wife complained about it. That's all I know about it. My brothers give money and presents to my parents. That's how they buy them off.

Inasmuch as I'm not like other people, since I have an abnormal sexuality, I prefer to keep to myself. For some years I haven't had any sexual relationships. Just fantasies. I miss being sexual. I feel it's not normal, not to have sex, not to be loved by someone who feels I'm worth it. I find it difficult to imagine what the future holds for me.

CHAPTER SEVEN

From Nightmares to Fantasies:
Coping Strategies and Life Scripts

At the cognitive and affective levels, a boy who has been sexually abused must in one way or another adapt to the traumas he has undergone. His own response will depend, among other things, on the reaction of his immediate family to his disclosure of the abuse, on the type of abuse involved, the circumstances that produced it, its frequency, its duration, and other significant events that took place before, during, and after the abuse. One thing seems certain: the traumas linked to sexual abuse create certain cognitive connections in the child's or young adolescent's mind. That is why boys and men who have been sexually abused are inevitably affected by it, although not all are affected in the same way. The aggression they have suffered has brought them knowledge of emotions, sensations, gratifications, revulsions, anguish, and suffering that will remain part of their life experience and will shape their way of constructing reality.

One must not lose sight of the fact, however, that a learning experience does not necessarily denote a determined cooperation on the part of the learner. On the contrary, the learning derived from most experiences is acquired in an involuntary manner, be it through imitation of adults or of peers, or through gradual adaptation to situations whose disagreeable aspects must be minimized. Childhood and adolescence are justly recognized as key periods in human learning because the brain, still developing, stores new material more readily in those years and thus establishes lasting cognitive connections. In this way certain boys will come to associate sexuality with suffering, desire with what is forbidden, sexual arousal with feelings of guilt, etc.

All the respondents in my study emphasized one thing: after the abuse they were never the same. Something in them had shifted. Their perceptions and their way of living have incorporated, in some way, the "lessons" learned from the sexual abuse and the events surrounding it. In her work *Trauma and Recovery*,[1] psychiatrist Judith Herman maintains that a particularly traumatizing event causes a revision of the victim's ideas about human relationships: attachment, trust, friendship, love, the sense of community. In the child or adolescent, this traumatizing shock can brutally upset the development omit of identity and the building of a sense of security. It will also turn topsy turvy the value system on which the meaning of life is built and may even go as far as to destroy belief in a divine or natural order of things to which a young person may be attached, plunging him into a deep existential crisis.

Perceptions and life strategies develop from the memories and expectations of each individual. Ex-victims of sexual abuse are no exception to the rule. Their memories of troubling or traumatic experiences may thus be used to orient their conduct towards adapting to these experiences, if not to exorcising them. These are what I will term, in the following pages, their "coping strategies." They include, both consciously and unconsciously, lifestyle scenarios that, like film scripts, set out what will be required on the levels of the emotions, love, and sexuality in order to adapt to the context of sexual abuse and its aftermath.

The ex-victims of sexual abuse are likely to generate rather precise strategies to cope with the after-effects of their traumatic experience. These strategies often involve scripting relationships in an effort to preserve their mental equilibrium or restore their identity. The term "coping," however, does not imply any sense of "making better." On the contrary, in trying to adapt to their traumatisms or to become free of them, some former abuse victims will, as time goes by, get into deeper trouble or unleash dramas just as grave as those they are trying to put behind them.

The various strategies we will examine are not always obvious to the boys and grown-up former victims. Not that they are unaware of what they are doing, but they are sometimes the last to become aware of the dynamics of the relationships in which they are involved. Six patterns of conduct emerge from the respondent's stories, but these strategies are not necessarily exclusive.

Many of the boys and men I questioned have moved from one pattern to another during the course of their evolution. What is more, some boys have moved through virtually all six of the strategies at different times in their lives.

The interpretation of human strategies supposes that all human behaviour is oriented towards results, depending upon the capacity to rationalize, the presence of possibility, and a way of manœuvering.[2] Human beings, especially youngsters, only rarely have a perfectly clear and conscious idea of what it is they are trying to accomplish. Through experiment they discover that, in a specific context, certain strategies bring better results than others. In short, they adapt themselves to the behaviours of others and to different situations but not in a completely planned manner as the idea of strategy might suggest. It is by means of trial and error and through an imprecise, partial, and subjective understanding of a given situation that adaptive or coping strategies are worked out. Whether the desired results are effectively attained or not will be considered further in the last chapter of this work.

"IT'S FATE": THE VICTIM STRATEGY

The life stories of some boys suggest that they continue to find themselves in the position of victim. Sometimes it involves situations in which the young man will again tolerate abuse without denouncing it or attempting to escape it. He is convinced that his being abused goes without saying, that to be sexually exploited is part of life, at least part of his life. This is termed *passive revictimization*. In other cases a young man seems to put himself, more or less deliberately, in the dangerous position of being again exploited or aggressed sexually. It is as though he runs recklessly into relationships that remind him in one way or another of the abuse to which he has already been subjected. This is termed *active revictimization*.

When boys who have been sexually victimized find themselves working as prostitutes or as sexual escorts or nude dancers, for example, it is likely that their past abuse has triggered certain cognitive connections that recognize sexuality as a means of obtaining something they want, be it attention from adults, money, drugs, clothes, gifts, etc. These young men have often assimilated at a very young age the principle of giving in order to get something.

In receiving material or emotional rewards in return for sexual acts, they have learned a lesson they will remember. They may also, from now on, repeat the traumatizing experience of the past in such a way as to render it commonplace. Replaying the same scenario over and over seems to reassure and comfort them with the feeling that such behaviour cannot be so serious after all, and, since they themselves are making the decision to offer their sexuality, they are now masters of the situation. At least this is the impression they have. Thus, Eric, twenty-three years old, sexually abused from the age of six by the father of a foster family, states: "From the time I was quite little, I was obliged to go with men. To begin with, I didn't even understand, but I must have learned to like it somehow. When I get up in the morning, the first thing I think about is getting ready to look for clients, like it's become a reflex. Even when the guys ask me to do the most disgusting things, it doesn't upset me that much any more. In any case, I wouldn't know what else to do to earn money."

Steve, twenty-five years old and sexually aggressed by two adolescents at the age of five, explains: "Clients? I do it for the the cash, for drugs. For me, it's not a question of liking men but of profiting from them like they do from me. I prefer girls, but they don't pay."

As it has for these two respondents, sexual abuse often serves as a training ground for prostitution. According to the Canadian Badgley Commission's report on sexual abuse of children, seventy-seven percent of male child prostitutes had their first sexual relations by the age of twelve or earlier. In one case out of three it occurred in a context of violence and in less than one case in four the context was incest.[3] Some American studies double the latter statistic.[4] It seems that a victim of sexual abuse, having become accustomed to it, is all the more willing to take on the role of sexual object. A boy who has been been treated as a sex slave over a period of years can take refuge in what he knows: a world of dependence, submission, humiliation, even of brutalization. Some have a tendency to deny their own emotional or sexual needs and adopt a fatalist philosophy: "If I want to be loved or appreciated, I have to provide sex, whether I want it or not." This reasoning could explain why for some young men, "pleasuring the other" sexually is an absolute priority, never mind their own desire (or lack of it) or their own satisfaction.

"Once a victim, always a victim" seems to be the reaction of formerly abused boys who come to see as commonplace the difficult situations in which they all too often find themselves. They envisage their destiny as predetermined, believe they are doomed to it, and see themselves as the playthings of others. Those who have been sexually abused by several adults, or for long periods of time, are especially inclined to entertain such thoughts. Their resignation can no doubt be explained by the fact that the abuses they have endured have sapped their ability to believe in the possibility of their ever directing their own lives. "After what has happened to me, what do you want me to do?" This essentialist perception of themselves – as though, from their point of view, they were born to suffer – is probably at the source of a great number of escapist and desperate behaviours such as self-mutilation, sexual compulsivity, dependence on toxic substances or toxic relationships. Having lost all hope, these young people are also among the most suicidal.

It is possible that in taking refuge in a familiar psychological or relational attitude – the attitude that prevailed during the abuse – certain boys feel themselves paradoxically to be safer. They cling to their victim status because the unknown scares them. An unhappy destiny may be perceived as a defence against a fate that may be even worse. By this stage, certain children or adolescents have been so deprived on the emotional level, or so mistreated on the physical level, that their world hardly comprises anything beyond the array of tormented experiences they have always known.

WHO WILL BE NEXT?
THE FRONTIER RUNNER STRATEGY

Whatever reason a boy may give afterwards, he has crossed a boundary, a forbidden frontier, when he inflicts upon another child what he himself went through, when he inveigles a child into the prohibited area in which he found himself in the past: the zone of sexual abuse, silence, and secrets.

As I have already stressed, actively reproducing an abuse that was once passively endured is without doubt aimed at repairing the past since this time the experience becomes a source of pleasure. In reliving the traumatic experience by reversing roles and identifying himself up to a point with the aggressor, the adolescent or grown-up former victim is attempting to protect his personal sense of masculinity. He takes the "best role," from his point of view, in the relationship of power that plays out between a sexually abused child and an abuser. This would explain why ex-victims who become abusers display hardly any empathy towards their victim: they certainly do not wish to imagine themselves in his shoes. It is a situation they are pointedly trying to forget.

Boys who come to identify with the aggressor in this way lose less self-esteem, at least to begin with, so that temporarily their sense of identity survives the abuse experience more easily. If the important thing for a male is to maintain his virility, superiority, or dominance, then the greatest disgrace is to be sexually subjugated by another male. Thus, affirming their virility is a matter of urgency for many masculine victims of sexual abuse, and committing abuse is unfortunately perceived as one way to bring this about. It is an attempt to liberate the self from trauma by actively repeating what was once passively endured. Therapists who work with child abusers confirm that, in many cases, the latter reproduce their own victimization by going after children who are roughly the same age that they themselves were when first abused. Indeed, aggressors often see themselves in the children they abuse. But they rewrite their own history in order symbolically to come through as winners this time around.

Most respondents confided that they had fantasized about abusing. Approximately one-third of them acted on their fantasies or tried to realize them at least once. Some of them quickly came to reverse their role as victim after having been sexually abused themselves. Thus, Marcel was only fourteen years old when he sexually abused his little brother, aged five, and his little sister aged six. As for Paul, at ten years old he began, while babysitting, to touch the genitals of his brother's baby girls. Jean-Marc, at sixteen, began sexually interfering with a little neighbour. With Pascal, at seventeen, it was the little girl who lived in the same foster home with him. Vladimir, although still an adolescent, was a procurer of under-age prostitutes.

That a certain number of male adolescents or adults who have suffered sexual abuse as children may in turn adopt similar behaviours should not lead to the generalized and erroneous belief that those who have been abused will inevitably become abusers themselves. We should understand, rather, that ex-victims

who sexually abuse others are seeking, albeit misguidedly, a resolution to the abuse they experienced in the past. They feel they
are salvaging the masculininty or the power they lost at the hands
of their aggressor. Committing abuse may therefore seem to them
like a return to a "fair" balance. "What I was made to suffer I have
the right to do to someone else."

Following the example of his own aggressor and disregarding
the negative fall-out from his own past experience, the adolescent
ex-victim who sexually abuses a younger child may see himself
more as an initiator than an abuser. Some children come to see
forced sex as so ordinary that they don't question it, even once
they are no longer being abused. Abused boys may also have
acquired a certain repertoire of sexual reactions and behaviours.
A precocious and drawn-out participation in sexual activity, even
when not desired, can lead a child or an adolescent to eroticize
certain aspects of it. This involuntary apprenticeship is all the
more effective since the child has hardly any ability to understand
his own sexuality, far less to manage it.

Victims can become habituated and desensitized to sexual
abuse, especially if the abuse they were subjected to was repetitive. In spite of himself, a boy victim of sexual abuse may have
learned to associate sexual pleasure with the dehumanization of
both participants. Paradoxically, his aggressor's acts may serve as
a positive reinforcement: "If he gets what he wants when he goes
after it like that, why couldn't I do the same?" After all, the
aggressor seems to come out of it the winner, without having to
explain himself and without being punished – which is frequently
the case: very few of the aggressors of the boys interviewed had
ever been made to suffer the consequences of their acts. Since the
perpetrator of the abuse is often a man who has held a significant
place in the life of the boy, it is even possible that he may remain
a role model. Are not pre-adolescents, generally, urged to learn
from their elders?

Some of the ex-victims' testimony is a good illustration of the
situation described above. Maxim, twenty-three years old, was
sexually abused as a child and then tried as an adolescent to abuse
his brother of eight years. He relates: "I hardly gave it any
thought. It seemed normal to me to ask him to suck me off. It had
been done to me so often." Marcel, now seventeen, a victim of
sexual abuse perpetrated by a neighbour when he was six to eight
years old, afterwards violated his younger brother and sister:

"There are some things you've found pleasant in all of that," he said. "You're tempted to repeat it, to want to know what it feels like." On the other hand, Paul, abused by several members of his family from the time he was five until he reached twenty-four years of age, finds no other explanation for the abuse committed against his young nieces apart from curiosity and "liberation": in short, he changed places with the aggressor.

"SOMEBODY HAS TO PAY FOR IT": THE AVENGER STRATEGY

The behaviour of the avenger resembles that of the frontier runner, except that what motivates the avenger to commit abuse, whether it be physical or sexual, is neither curiosity, mere indifference, nor re-establishing his manliness but, quite simply, pure vengeance. To subject another person to what he has gone through can certainly imply a vindictive intention on the part of an abused boy. Psychoanalyst Robert Stoller, in trying to understand the vengeance component of sexual excitation among his patients, writes: "Sexual excitement is most likely to be set off at the moment when adult reality resembles the childhood trauma or frustration ... anticipation of danger ... is experienced as excitement, a word used not to describe voluptuous sensations so much as a rapid vibration between fear of trauma and hope of triumph ... The central theme that permits this advance to pleasure is revenge. It reverses the positions of the actors in the drama and so also reverses their affects. One moves from victim to victor."[5]

Unlike the "frontier runner" previously described, the avenger who commits sexual abuse will prefer to select children who do not resemble himself. In his wish to pervert or to defile someone else, he will generally target "the ideal child," beaming, confident, popular: in short, the child he himself would have wanted to be had the drama he went through not taken place.[6] The boy victim of sexual abuse has heard so often that he risks doing the same thing later on that the prophecy haunts and disturbs him. Those who have received help and protection following childhood sexual abuse appear notably less at risk than others in this respect. Conversely, those who have continued to live in a climate of stress, secrecy, and guilt are at greater risk of becoming avengers, although nothing can be taken for granted in this respect.

This seeking of vengeance is not found only in an exact reproduction of what the victim has experienced. For example, anger
and resentment may be expressed through vandalism, physical
violence, or prostitution that involves exploiting the client through
theft. Eric, twenty-three years old, sometimes feels that when he
acts as a prostitute he makes his clients suffer, dominates them
and makes them pay, literally, for what other men inflicted on him
in the prime of his youth. Seventeen-year-old Francis, siding with
a group of skinheads, participated actively in punitive trips to the
gay village in Montreal to beat up homosexuals. Other boys have
told how they committed delinquent acts almost without remorse,
because they felt they were making society pay for what they had
been forced to endure.

The vengeance strategy is rarely directed toward the real
aggressors of the past, who are often out of reach. Vengeance is
carried out rather on those who, in the mind of the adolescent or
young adult, personify their abuser for one reason or another:
certain types of men, individuals suspected of having homosexual
or bisexual tendencies, people representing authority, etc. The
rebellion of some young male victims of sexual abuse is thus
aimed at an exterior world perceived as menacing, exploitative,
unjust, or dangerous.

The avenger's strategy is not only carried out on strangers he
likens to the aggressor: it is also carried out in everyday life, on
close family or even on loved ones. In many cases, it is those who
care for him, his friends or his lovers, who are targeted by the ex-
victim in search of revenge. That is why so many of them find
themselves saddled with problems of violence in their intimate
relationships. "Somebody has to pay." What is more, the avenging
tactic, whether forced sex, verbal abuse, blackmail, threats, disparagement, physical violence, etc., will often create a spreading
stain on the life of the ex-victim who has more or less consciously
adopted it. Equal to the pain he feels, his anger is inextinguish-
able. He must attack "the other" before he himself is attacked.

LIKE BATMAN AND ROBIN: THE RESCUER STRATEGY

It is striking to see the lengths to which some boy victims of abuse
will go, later on, to form a close relationship with a man of similar

age to that of their abuser. It is as though they tell themselves that this one, at least, will be able to love them "properly," will rescue them in a way and, possibly, help them in turn to become rescuers. It must be understood that, in a child who has been abused, the entire relational system has most likely been disturbed, creating the certainty of isolation. The youngster will thus, sooner or later, attempt to rebuild significant emotional ties. This is the moment when what I call the Batman and Robin syndrome makes its appearance.

Everyone knows Batman and Robin, those comic book heroes who later went on to television and movie fame. They form an inseparable pair, the elder serving as mentor to the younger. Now, the Batman and Robin duo is the model of the ideal relationship that numerous abused boys more or less consciously seek. They are on the lookout for a protective, even restorative, relationship with an older man. A very close relationship with a reassuring figure appeals to them as a way to take care of their wounded masculinity, to regain trust in both themselves and in others. What greater positive victory over fate could there be, really, than to meet an older person who would, this time, protect them. Frequently, a relationship like that of Batman and Robin aims at compensating an abused boy for a former loss: the loss of a father, an uncle, a friend, or a big brother – whether or not this person is the abuser – who in the past had seemed to love him before abandoning him. Certain abused youngsters hope to find the recognition shown them by their aggressors before their real intentions surfaced.

In the years following the abuse, and in spite of certain apprehensions, several of the respondents had such a privileged relationship with an adult. Their goal, more or less admittedly, was to find in this man a role model and guide (as Batman is to Robin) whom they would admire in return (just as Robin admires Batman).

The problem is that the search for a mentor does not bring an end to their mistrust, still less to their ambivalence towards adults: once bitten, twice shy. The higher the youngster's expectations of an adult in whom he has invested all his hopes, the greater the risks of again being let down. This time, the least false step, the smallest slip, appears like a new abandonment or betrayal. True heroes being rare, the young boy's idyllic dream will only rarely come to pass. One can imagine the drama when the adult shows himself to be incapable of shouldering the role that has been foisted on him. His pupil, rightly or wrongly, comes to believe that he recognizes in him another exploiter.

To be appreciated and loved for himself alone and not for his body is what most men who have been victims of sexual abuse in childhood long for. In a way, what most frightens the ex-victim is what most attracts him: a man who will love him truly for himself alone. With such a man the ex-victim believes he can transform the promiscuity that caused him so much pain during the abuse into a real intimacy; he will turn the enslavement into a relationship of equals. His masculinity having been called into question, he counts on re-establishing it through a friendship that will manifest a virile companionship. However, this particular type of friendship also presents difficulties, if not hazards.

The sexually abused male child or adolescent may, in spite of himself, establish relationships that favour his renewed exploitation. This is all the more likely if he has a tendency to fall back on the seductive behaviour precociously learned in the context of abuse. Some respondents have been cruelly disappointed to learn that their rescuer might be interested in them on a sexual level. Not all adults are potential aggressors but the motivations of an older person who wraps himself in the Batman costume are not always clear. He too carries a certain amount of baggage; no one knows what is hidden behind the mask of the hero.

Some adolescent or young adult respondents, especially if they are of a homosexual or bisexual orientation, will view their privileged relationship with such adults as not excluding mutually satisfying sexual relations, while others are allergic to any contact that might suggest a sexual relationship or, worse, provoke a context of abuse. In each case, relationship is meant to obliterate the past; the young people intend to prove to themselves that men are not all the same, since at least one of them has been able to show them sincere affection.

About one-third of the respondents had been at one time in a Batman and Robin type of relationship. If in some cases the rescuer strategy resulted in setbacks, if not in repeated traumas, in other situations the results were happier. But such relationships can be full of pitfalls, and for good reason. Because of the confused emotions they have acquired, ex-victims of sexual aggression often experience a certain ambivalence on the emotional level. What they admire one day they may detest the next. For example, some deplore the emotional dependence inherent in the symbiotic relationship they have sought out. Others, having offered sexual relations to an adult who is important to them, regret the latter's positive response to their advances: once again, they see themselves as exploited or betrayed, since love has only been extended to them in order to take advantage of their body.

A mixture of trust and mistrust somehow results in an abused boy's readily suspecting that all adults have a hidden agenda: to take advantage of him or to abuse him. Countering such an impression is all the more difficult to do since, in his wish to exorcise the past, the young man will sometimes seek out, consciously or not, relationships that resemble those he had with his abuser, with all the risks and disillusionment this entails.

To complete the parallel with Batman and Robin, it is essential to point out how much many ex-victims dream of becoming "rescuers" of other children. Among the respondents of working age, a number have indeed chosen careers in the helping or teaching professions. All these men spoke of great satisfaction in being able to give what they were unable to receive: the reassuring attention of an adult. Sometimes, however, the fear that they might themselves commit abuse has held them back from fulfilling their aspirations. "I would have liked to work with youngsters, but it was so impressed upon me that those who are abused become abusers that I didn't want to take any risks," said one respondent who hesitated for a long time before going into teaching at the primary level, a profession in which today he finds great satisfaction. Several men wanted to work with other victims of physical or sexual abuse. Some have, in one way or another, realized this plan. While such an attitude is the opposite of the avenger's desire for "an eye for an eye," it probably has the same origin. It speaks of the same need to wipe out the past, to reinvent the world.

EROTICIZING DIFFERENT ELEMENTS OF ABUSE: THE DAREDEVIL STRATEGY

Since the process of being traumatized involved the experience of learning about sex, it is not surprising to find certain elements of abuse in the sexuality of some victims. The secrecy, forbidden acts, exhibitionist nudity, the danger of being discovered in illegal situations, for example, tend to be eroticized. By incorporating such aspects of their abuse into their own fantasies or sexual relations, these ex-victims, boys or men, may transform the earlier trauma into pleasure. What was painful can be transformed into a source of euphoria and the tensions provoked by risk can become a source of sexual arousal.

Thus, the exhibitionism some respondents engage in can be one way of rendering less fearsome, or making seem more ordinary, the nudity forced upon them by their aggressor. Some respondents allude to situations where they have taken pleasure in having sexual relations in front of witnesses, masturbating in front of strangers (for example in parks or public toilets, or in view of the windows of women living alone), or in making erotic photos or dancing nude. That this theme recurs so often, although initially there was no question on this topic, suggests that it may be a relatively well known practice among male victims of sexual abuse in childhood. The question also arises as to whether exhibitionism (that is, imposing one's sexuality on someone else as the aggressor did in the past) is not, at least in certain cases, another way to commit an aggression, albeit solely on a psychological level.

The erotic connotations that attach to what is forbidden often manifest themselves in recurring intrusive images. Scenes or practices associated with past abuses then come constantly to mind but with erotic overtones. This is the case with certain sadomasochistic practices. Causing pain to the partner during sex means seeking to dominate or to feel that one is dominating. Some ex-victims are stupefied to see themselves reproducing, in the context of their present consensual sexual or love relationships, sexual acts that formerly disgusted them. These young men seem to demonstrate through their apparent temerity in matters sexual that one of the strategies allowing a coming to terms with the abuse is to integrate some of its aspects into erotic practices.

Many boys who have been sexually abused have never learned to recognize any limits whatsoever on the sexual level, since their aggressor so blithely went beyond them. The abuse they experienced revealed to them an adult sexuality they describe as "primitive" and "out of control." For some, sexuality seems to be the shadow side of the human being, a zone in which the most uncontrollable instincts are manifest.

In their anguish at seeing their sexuality modelled on that of their abuser, some young people are apt to go from one extreme to another: from shamelessness to the strictest modesty, from celibacy to multiple partners. So it was with Francis, who made a "chastity belt" for himself, wearing it under several layers of clothing so that his father might not totally undress him. However, after drinking or doing drugs at parties, this same adolescent was apt to play the role of exhibitionist. In the same fashion, Bruno would go from declaring he was homophobic to displaying sexually provocative behaviour around men, frequently visiting areas known as homosexual pick-up spots. Several respondents made it clear that their sex life was given over to the most varied practices: they would alternate being disgusted by sexuality to being insatiable, even compulsive. What was forbidden would now take one form, now the opposite.

The eroticization of what was secret or forbidden seems to be associated with behaviour learned within the framework of abuse and thus reinforces the age-old tie between sexuality and taboo. One can imagine that repeated sexual abuse of a child by an adult constitutes such an invasion of the child's integrity that the relationship of the youngster to his own body will later pose a problem: he no longer knows what it is he hopes for, how far he can go, what are the limits. At different stages in his life the same individual may be sickened and disgusted by sexuality, now obsessed by it; now homophobic, now homosexual; now abstinent, now a Don Juan. But he is always dissatisfied, because he does not really know what it is he desires or what is good or bad for him.

LOOKING NORMAL:
THE CONFORMIST STRATEGY

In his novel *The Conformist*, author Alberto Moravia[7] describes the life of Marcel, a young victim of sexual touching who by accident kills his abuser and thereafter tries to blot out the double memory of the aggression and of the murder by proving to all that he is "like everyone else." Like Marcel, the ex-victim who opts for conformity tends not only to deny what has happened to him but also to model his conduct on what he thinks is close to the most conventional of "normal appearances."

Matthew, who was almost eighteen years old when I interviewed him, is a good example of this strategy. His self-assurance cannot disguise his insecurity when he is faced with any reference to homosexuality or to masculine vulnerability. Vladimir presents an even more conclusive case: as early as adolescence, he becomes a pimp for a network of young girls he recruits from among his girlfriends. He plays tough and acts like a real Don Juan, but deep down he is asking himself whether perhaps he is homosexual. In the evenings, while his "girls" are working, he walks past gay bars telling himself he should perhaps try his luck and go inside. Behind his well-built macho image hides an insecure youngster who is ambivalent about his sexual orientation. Boys like Vladimir could even be described as having a heterosexual façade that serves to scare off any possibility of homosexual relations – which they have involuntarily encountered in their abuse and which, to a certain point, they have now eroticized.

According to some Freudian writers, among them Serge Tisseron, the victim of a seduction often internalizes the contradictory characteristics of his seducer. In particular, he may have appropriated the shame of the seducer and acquired the idea that he, the victim, was responsible for his seducer's arousal and also for the seduction.[8] As a result, some young men, like little Marcel in Moravia's novel, will do whatever it takes to erase from their lives, their appearance, and their behaviour whatever had interested the man who abused them. Unlike those who become exhibitionists, for example, they try to fade into the background, to remain unseen, even to make themselves ugly by self-mutilation, or by deliberately starving themselves to become skinny or overeating to become obese. They go out of their way to prove to themselves and show to others that they are not in the least the kind of person who could be abused, that the abuse ought never to have happened and, therefore, could never have happened.

Within this quest for conformity a certain homophobia very often shows up. Being "normal" males, that is to say exclusively heterosexual, they claim to be sickened by homosexuals and their practices. Nevertheless, beyond this ostentatious rejection of homosexuality, obvious but guilt-provoking homosexual practices sometimes appear. Obsession with appearing "normal," which in Western culture tends to exclude homosexuality, guides the reactions of numerous respondents who are actually homosexual or bisexual. Bruno, for example, despite his squarely homophobic stance, appears to have more homosexual than heterosexual encounters. The same goes for Eric, who prostitutes himself exclusively with men. Although he declares himself to be probably more straight than gay, he has had scarcely any heterosexual relationships. The case of Justin, now twenty-four, is also instructive. He has spent years cultivating a "normal appearance" as a good husband and family man, while battling in vain against homosexual attractions. His guilt is magnified in his mind since he associates such tendencies with a loss of self-control. Some respondents, particularly the younger ones, insist on labelling themselves exclusivly heterosexual, betraying a need to reassure themselves of a certain normality, or at least what they perceive as normality at this point in their lives.

The conformist is the most inclined of all to deny what has happened to him and that may be how he really sees it. Of course, it is difficult to tell whether the amnesia, partial or total, experienced by some respondents in the years following their abuse results from a conscious strategy or not. As a defence mechanism, however, it has allowed them to forget the abuse they suffered or to minimize its after-effects for a period of time. Some men have been in therapy for years before realizing that the symptoms they were trying in vain to repress were linked to buried memories of sexual abuse that had occurred decades earlier.

Strategies that allow victims to cope with the aftermaths of sexual abuse may take many forms. I have sketched only the most common. Moreover, these strategies are not mutually exclusive. A boy or man may well proceed from one to another. As contradictory or paradoxical as they may appear, all strategies aim at the restoration of a certain equilibrium in the individual who puts them to work. Although they may later seem ineffective, all strategies at one time or another have seemed to act as a salve on the traumatising wounds of abused boys. It would be beneficial to recognize these tactical patterns for what they are, if only to help male victims of sexual abuse understand their behaviour and, if necessary, work out alternative solutions.

It is important to emphasize that the strategies adopted by young male ex-victims to attenuate or exorcise the aftermaths of sexual abuse do not necessarily lead to problematic behaviours. These tactics are not necessarily deployed in their most extreme forms. There are rescuers, daredevils, and conformists who will never make trouble for anyone, themselves included. And strategies are sometimes carried out in a very subtle way, through acts that are on the whole anodyne but nonetheless profoundly meaningful to the person undertaking them. Ultimately, only the significance given by the individual to his behaviour can help to determine what strategies the behaviours represent.

Justin, thirty-four years old, was an incest victim from a very young age. It involved his father, his uncle, and his older brother.

I only remembered recently, when I began to analyze my behaviours, my problem with commitment, my fear of men, even when I love them and when they are good to me. I was sexually abused by my father when I was four years old and then a bit later by my uncle. Afterwards, it was my brother. He was four years older than I was.

My father was the first. He left home after that, went into a depression. At least, that's what they told me. He was put in a psychiatric institution. They told me he was given electric shock treatment. I think my mother discovered us together. What I remember about it is that it was the first time my father was being affectionate towards me. He was usually quite brutal with me. Some memories remain: he shut me in the garage and chased me. Another time he was sitting in the car. His penis was out. He had an erection. It happened about four or five times, I think, between the time I was four until the time I was seven. Each time, he got something from me by using his authority over me, not by being violent. It's a type of control, or manipulation. After all, he was my father, so I obeyed him. There was no penetration but there was ejaculation, in my mouth probably. I've always been afraid of sperm since then; still am today. Is it because of the traumatic experiences with my father or with my uncle? It's difficult to say, because my uncle moved in with us around the same time, when I was between five and six years old. He'd just left his wife. He too disappeared from the house overnight. He lived in the base-ment. He used to touch me and ask me to touch him. I was afraid of him. I knew it wasn't normal. With my father it was different, maybe because there was a certain innocence about it. It was like a game. Not with my uncle. With him it was gross.

I'm trying to recall that period in time, but it isn't easy. I remember I had become the sort of child who accepts love from anyone at all and who would have done just about anything to be loved. I came from a dysfunctional family: there wasn't much love; we didn't talk to each other; there was a climate of

tension. I paid for peace and quiet by trying to please everyone. I was completely without identity. All that counted was
getting people to love me. Right up until I reached seventeen
I was Daddy's good little boy or the little girl Mummy had
never had, because I was somewhat effeminate compared to my
brothers. And, wouldn't you know, all this to overcome the fear
my parents would separate. That's probably one of the reasons
I never told anyone about what happened with my father.
Never. My mother never learned anything from me. Even today,
I ask myself if my mother really knew what was going on with
my father and my uncle.

In spite of everything, I was always smiling when I was little. I can tell from photos. But inside I felt bad. It's like I had
two personalities. On the outside I was a good little boy, steady,
good at school. Inside, I felt different from the others. I was
apprehensive.

Towards the age of six, I heard the word "fag" for the first
time. My father would often say to me: "If you don't do such
and such, you'll look like a fag." I didn't know what it was but
I knew it wasn't right, something that wasn't good. And then at
home, they quickly identified me with that. At school, apparently, they were calling me a fag: I was thin, a bit delicate,
which is never okay for a boy. I didn't know what a fag was,
but I didn't want to be one.

My other personality, the one that developed secretly, was the
little boy who looked more and more at other boys, who appreciated how beautiful they are. But I couldn't really get hold of
that desire … I pushed it away. I chose not to be like that. The
other personality took over. I remember my father telling me
one time when I ran away from a gang of boys who were fighting: "Don't run like that, you look like a sissy!" I was humiliated. From that day on I decided to be a chameleon. I learned
to play a game.

When I was thirteen or fourteen my older brother and
I began having sex. It all began when we were fooling around,
wrestling. We were all over each other. I don't know how it
came about, but at a certain point our pants came down …
I wasn't forced. I didn't see it as abusive. Only later did I realize that he had tricked my emotions, that he had exploited my
need for affection. I still have after-effects today of that betrayal.

It was the third contact I'd had with a man in my life; in all three cases it was a form of incest and at that point I still hadn't gone out with a girl.

In sexual relations with my brother, funnily enough, he was passive and I was the active one, the one who pleasured him, in other words. He participated very little, except to make the first move. He knew I was turned on by looking at him, seeing his body. He knew how to get to me. He became my idol. It was the first time I felt any affection for any male; my father used to criticize me all the time. When my brother left to get married, it proved to me that I couldn't trust any man. It was a huge blow. We had been having sex for three years, regularly.

I say I loved him, but apart from our sexual activity we didn't talk that much. To tell the truth, he wasn't really present in my life. It was only during the actual act of sex that he showed me any love. At the time I was more or less conscious of it. Just like I was more or less conscious that I was interested in men. But that was quite simply not an option. You get married and you have children: that's what men do. My brother was a good example of that.

Around sixteen, I became interested in women. I met one girl, then another. I'm aware that I programmed myself to make love to them, to ejaculate. And I became quite good at pleasuring a woman. I learned how to obtain pleasure and how to give it. As for homosexuality, I had to forget it. My wife, even today, doesn't believe I have always been gay. She reminds me I was always having erections, that we made love every day easily ... But I know ...

So then, around eighteen, I met the mother of my children. I had already begun drinking. Alcohol gives me the courage, the self-assurance to go ahead. I met my wife at my brother's wedding. It was a lucky chance. Quite quickly, she expressed her love for me. It was the first time a woman told me she loved me. I was her Prince Charming. She's very pretty, sensual, rich, popular. I climbed the social ladder, since her family was well off. But after two years of going together I left her because I was afraid to commit. I got drunk like never before. I called her a few days later. She succeeded in persuading me to get together again. I was afraid of being alone, of being rejected by my parents and my friends. And then, homosexuality is still associated with the betrayal of my brother. Around this time, my mother became sick with cancer. She was really the only person who meant anything to me. I promised God, if she survived, I would be the perfect boy she dreamed of. I offered my life to save hers.

At twenty, I got married. Home life went well for the first few years. My reticence disappeared. Everything went well, thanks to my wife's parents, who helped us and included us in their influential social circle. I remember, though, that on our wedding day, in the bath, I looked at my penis and told myself, "Now, my friend, forget that, you no longer have the right ..." I got out of the bath, got dressed and began to drink. My father was pissed off when he saw me like that. My wife was already used to it. For her, alcohol wasn't a problem, so long as I remained functional.

Just before the wedding, I confessed to my wife about my relationship with my brother. She told me what I wanted to hear, that it was just one step in the wrong direction, that it's all over. Very quickly, I felt pressured sexually. I had to drink to make love to her. I was never willing in the morning because I was sober; in the evening I began to drink quite early in order to get myself ready. I made her conform to my pace. I saw to it that I was always under the influence when we made love. I remember the first nights. We were living in a huge building. From one of the windows I could see a neighbour walking about naked. I would get up when my wife was asleep to look at him. That's what I found the most exciting. We were never alone in bed, my wife and I. Fantasies kept me company. The men who turned me on looked like my father, but mostly like my brother.

After a year we had a baby boy and after that a girl. I had become very busy professionally in order to provide properly for my family, but also in order to be out of the house. I felt guilty about this as far as my children were concerned. By now my wife had become more of a mother than a lover. She had become less demanding on the sexual level and that was fine with me. Me too, I was becoming more of a father than a lover. We were so wrapped up in our children that no one questioned the couple relationship.

After six years of marriage, I was the one who took a lover ... my brother-in-law, my wife's brother. It was like a continuation of the relationship I had had with my own brother. He's a bit older than me. We both do drugs and drink. One evening, he was drunk and so was I. I sensed I could take advantage of that. I made a move; he responded. We were at my place, in the basement. My wife was asleep upstairs with the kids. The alcohol helped as things unfolded. This went on for almost two years. We met more or less once a month. He was exactly like my brother, passive; he let me get on with it. I was the active one, I fellated him. Just like my brother, he considers himself completely heterosexual.

After that I went downhill quite rapidly. This man had reawakened something in me. I started cruising the park at night. My descent into hell began right there. My self-esteem dropped to zero. When I was drunk enough, I went out and got it on in the bushes with anyone who showed up. I went home very late. And the next day I'd be in shock, waking up beside my wife who'd say "Hi lover!" The children would get into bed with us: "Hi, Daddy!" I felt very bad.

One Christmas Eve, I was following a man in a shopping centre. He invited me to his place. I refused but regretted my decision. When I got home, I drank too much. I took off, ran away. I wanted to give it all up. I got on a bus without knowing where I was going. I phoned my wife so she wouldn't be worried. And then I told her everything, even about her brother. At first she refused to believe me, then she said if it was really like that then I'd never see my children again. I called my mother and asked if I could go live with her. She said I would be irresponsible if I left my family. So I went home as if nothing had happened. I stayed there for a whole year, drinking more and more. It was only a postponement.

One morning my daughter asked if that was wine in my glass. She told me it was too early to be drinking. Wow! She didn't yet know how to write her name but she knew her father was an alcoholic. That really got to me. I realized the impact my behaviour was having on the children. I left home for good. I made a suicide attempt. Then I looked for a therapist to cure my homosexuality. But instead he taught me to accept myself as

I am, to distinguish between abuse, compulsivity, and a balanced sexuality. Because, when all is said and done, I was no more at ease with homosexuality than I was with heterosexuality.

It's difficult for me to have a healthy view of homosexuality. The men I have loved have always abandoned me after using me. I used to be afraid, and still am afraid, of being loved. For a long time I made no distinction between my emotions, my affections, and my sexuality. It still isn't clear to me. I've recently become aware of how much I missed having a real father. I don't want to be like him, even if he has admitted that what he did was wrong and even if we now have a good relationship. It's the opposite of my relationship with my older brother, who doesn't speak to me, or hardly. I think he is afraid I'll reveal things about him, especially since I now accept that I'm gay. He doesn't spend much time with me. But my father seems to have forgotten what went on after all the shock treatments he's had.

I recently decided to move so that I could live closer to my children. I've left my job to be nearer to them. I don't want them to be without a father. I don't want them to be messed up later on, like me. I'm aware of how the abuse has affected my life, and I didn't want to pass that on to my own children.

I realize I have never lived a really human relationship, something more than just sexual, with a man or a woman. For a long time I saw myself as heterosexual. After I accepted it, I regarded myself as homosexual. On the emotional level, I think I'm more bisexual because I like being with women just as much as being with men. There's a difference between having sex standing up and being at ease with someone. Being at ease with someone, male or female, is a bit like making love with your heart.

Today I have many friends, men and women, and this is important if I want to come through this. My shame at having lived the life I've had, and being who I am, is gradually lessening. It's the fear of intimacy, of commitment, that's difficult to conquer. I'm working on it. Despite the problems it's given me, I think my sexual orientation would be the same, with or without the sexual abuse. Maybe the problem is that the incest prevented me from calmly discovering my own sexuality right from the start.

CHAPTER EIGHT

To Turn the Page or to Rewrite It?
Prevention and Intervention

While conducting my research, three questions were asked repeatedly both by respondents and by colleagues with whom I shared my observations: Is it possible to oneself extricate from the after-effects of sexual abuse? What is it that distinguishes ex-victims who seem to be "coming out of it" from the others? How can we better help boys who have undergone sexual abuse?

The many types of abuse and their after-effects call for a large array of interventions, which I cannot completely cover here. I do not pretend to reinvent social intervention in the area of sexual abuse. I would rather flesh out the conclusions that stem from my own research. In improving our understanding of the masculine experience of sexual abuse, will we not be better prepared to deal with it?

CAN SEXUAL ABUSE OF BOYS BE PREVENTED?

All childen, boys and girls, should learn to distinguish sexual molestation from sincere gestures of affection, and gratifying sexuality from exploitation. Whether this is learned at home, at school, or in other places where socialization occurs, such an education should emphasize not only the dangers of sexuality but also its positive aspects when explored within a context of respect for self and respect for others. Too often, parents or educators tackle the sexual side of life as though it were simply a question of issuing warnings, forgetting that a positive attitude to sexuality is necessary to personal equilibrium. The testimonies gathered within the framework of this research have clearly shown that sexual aggressors count upon the ignorance, the vulnerability, and the guilt of the boys they abuse. The dearth of education about love and sexuality is the accomplice of those who abuse children: the more naïve and resourceless the young people are, the easier prey they become.

Prevention campaigns are now tackling the question of family violence and sexual violence, but very little has been done specifically regarding the sexual abuse of boys. Many people believe that sexual abuse only happens to young girls. Recent works on rape or sexual exploitation ignore the reality of abuse beteween males or consider it to be very out of the ordinary. One sometimes has the impression that literature, television and cinema have in recent years examined the subject more thoroughly than the institutions charged with the protection of children. Public awareness of the existence of a masculine experience of sexual abuse is just beginning to emerge. A few initiatives could nonetheless accelerate things. For example, preventive messages regarding sexual abuse that are destined for young people might profitably point out the sexual aggressions boys are subjected to. It would also be of benefit to clearly identify the different types of sexual abuse: people are still reluctant to face up to the fact that in most cases of sexual aggression perpetrated against children, the abuser is a close relative.

Prevention campaigns should be directed not only at potential victims but also at those responsible for sexual abuse, that is to say, the potential aggressors and their accomplices. In sensitizing real or potential aggressors and the adults who protect them by their silence, we would be acting against the origin of the problem and not only on its consequences. Unfortunately, recidivism in this area is all too common, since so little attention is brought to these files. Frequently, a young man will bear witness to the fact that he was not the only one to be violated by the same individual. Far from it: the "score card" of certain child aggressors sometimes lists dozens, even hundreds of victims.

It is regrettable that the prospects of therapy for those who sexually exploit children are still very limited. Without doubt we are fooling ourselves if we think it possible to reorient the most profound desires of an individual, as some therapeutic approaches claim they can. Nevertheless, it is certain that adults, including aggressors, can be taught to manage their sexual desires in other ways and to control the manner in which they are expressed. In other words, even if an individual's fantasies cannot be changed, the individual can always learn to avoid vulnerable situations, control his conduct, and express his sexuality in ways that do not inflict injury or harm on others, especially children. Much has been said about antiandrogenic therapies to eliminate abusive behaviours (also described as chemical castration) these last few years, without posing the much more fundamental questions: Why do so many adults sexually abuse children? To what extent is this tendency irrepressible? Would it be possible to orient these adults towards other types of psychological or sexual gratification?

When it comes to prevention and even intervention in the area of sexual abuse, we are still in the stone age. There is a dearth of in-depth research concerning the profiles, dynamics, and motivations of child abusers and which types of therapeutic approach can successfully prevent recidivism. It should also be remembered that most acts of sexual aggression are committed by men who do not seem any different from others: they are the father, the older brother, the uncle, grandfather, friend of the family, neighbour, sitter, etc. When one hears of child abusers, the tendency is to think of men with long careers as paedophiles. We forget that many abusers do not have that type of profile.

The myth that paedophilia is an illness aims the spotlight on one very specific type of aggressor – the compulsive – but lifts the responsibility from men who commit such abuse, since it appears to be "stronger than they are." While working in this domain I have become convinced, on the one hand, that not all paedophiles will become child abusers, since they do not necessarily act on their desires, and, on the other hand, that not all child abusers are necessarily paedophiles. Actually, numerous aggressors seem to eroticize less the boy they are abusing than the type of relationship they have with him. Thus, certain among them will eroticize power, others will eroticize vulnerability, distress, transgression, and so on.

Assuredly, not all men are aggressors but all men should be better sensitized to the consequences of sexual abuse, because the problem is epidemic and in all social classes. It is essential that men who see themselves as potentially abusive should have access to specialized help. This help should be available to them before they abuse or before recidivism occurs. In this field, practically everything remains to be done. The feeble efforts agreed to thus far in no way correspond to the breadth of the problem.

Everything indicates that numerous child abusers have themselves been victims of sexual abuse during childhood. If we are to stop this production line of sexual abuse we must allow men hooked into the dynamic to acquire other ways of expressing their sexuality and playing out their erotic fantasies. The sexual education of aggressors, as that of their victims, is often inadequate. Some years ago I was consulted by a client who considered masturbation more reprehensible than the aggressions he had committed. This man had been sexually abused at the age of five, had committed his first sexual abuse at the age of sixteen, and had later repeated the offence numerous times, between short but frequent prison terms. Abusing was the only way of being sexual that he knew. During therapy in the past, no one was concerned, it seems, by the fact that he was lacking in the most elementary sexual education. Elimination of his desires and his abusive behaviours had been tried in vain, without taking into consideration the fact that he knew nothing else. Besides, rearranging his erotic fantasies in such a way that sexual relations with adults might be agreeable to him was not a simple matter: inside his adult body he was still a child for whom adults were all abusers.

Not all cases are as problematic. Nonetheless, in work with men who have committed sexual aggressions, understanding the origins and motivations of their conduct is primordial. Only a bringing to light of their own traumatisms will provide the starting point from which solutions may be sought, the prevention of recidivism being the absolute priority. Whatever their past may contain, these men often have in common that they are imprisoned by memories of past experiences and the damaging strategies they have adopted in the effort to escape their traumas. In the process, they have possibly transmitted them to others.

Taking the argument a notch further, I would say that the whole socialization of males is to be questioned with a view to preventing domination or aggression behaviours. One cannot value the exertion of power or domination, including on the sexual level, as an expression of virility while at the same time condemning it. Since aggressors have often themselves been sexually abused in childhood, or incited by the example of their peers or of their elders, the most useful tool for prevention is the education of and intervention with the younger generation. Prevention of sexual abuse, which could reproduce itself tomorrow, necessitates offering better living conditions and appropriate services to youngsters who are today sexually abused, battered, or rejected. They are the first victims of human violence and human stupidity: they will be among those most susceptible to finding, in bad solutions, a way to affirm or avenge themselves. In order to counter sexual violence, we must be able to propose something else as a solution to the problems of those who abuse. Violence, sexual or otherwise, is also a collective problem that calls for collective action, in which individuals as much as institutions should involve themselves. Institutions, rather than combatting this collective problem, seem to endorse it and make it seem commonplace. As I have tried to show, particularly in chapter 4, sexual abuse of boys is nothing but the symptom, if not the inheritance, of vast problems concerning relations between men, between generations, even between men and women.

It has been noted that all the abusive fathers described in this study had distant or strained relationships with their sons. Would an increased participation of men in the care of children bring with it a glimmer of hope in this regard? It is easier to be aggressive towards a child for whom one feels little empathy or affection. Men who come to learn a real tenderness in their relationships with their children will not confuse sexual abuse with affection. However, although real caring is a fine antidote to violence, it will not always suffice. That is why all measures that aim to render children less vulnerable before their elders, whoever they may be, should be encouraged. Such measures must especially include the development of children's rights and the ability of children to bear witness against adults without being intimidated or scared, whether by these adults or by an unfeeling judicial system. Knowing that he will be listened to and protected if he asks for help, an abused boy will be more inclined to break his silence. In according non-intimidating resources and rights to children and to adolescents, we shall be taking a step forward, since the present laws, although often excellent in theory, do not in practice have much weight. As supported by the numerous stories gathered here, aggressors often have the last word over their victims because, as adults, they know the weak points of the socio-judicial system and are able more easily to exploit or evade it.

The problem of false allegations of sexual abuse, which has been much talked about in the past few years, has no doubt worked against all abused children, although unjustified accusations remain the exception than the rule – about five percent of complaints, according to a review of the American literature.[1] Judges themselves show little empathy towards victims of sexual aggression, as the astonishing declaration by a Quebec judge recently indicated. She concluded that the sodomy practised on a small girl constituted a mitigating circumstance because it "preserved her virginity."[2] So long as the socio-judicial system does not facilitate the processing of complaints of sexual abuse against children, and so long as judges continue to treat such crimes flippantly, aggressors will believe themselves to be protected and children will not speak out.

Young victims are often intimidated by being asked to testify in public or to repeat their story time and time again. When the technical means and legal authorizations exist to record these testimonies one single time, and in private, it is unacceptable not to use such methods. Too many horror stories have been told by my respondents concerning their appearances in court to bear witness against their aggressors. To be accused of fabricating or lying certainly does not help a young victim who has gathered all his courage to make or to remake his testimony, to regain confidence in himself, and to rely on justice. Once again, the victim understands that the law of the jungle prevails.

WHEN SEXUAL ABUSE IS DISCLOSED

The cases reported throughout this work should render us more sensitive to the fact that the reactions of the people and institutions involved with the child are crucial for ending the abuse and reducing its aftermath. It is not rare, however, to find that the revelation of sexual aggression has not resulted in any action whatsoever to bring an end to the abuse and permit the victim to receive the help he requires. One might have hoped that the youngest respondents would have received more support than the older ones, in view of recent changes in the law and the evolution of attitudes. Nothing of the kind has transpired. Too often, still, the abusive act is denied, the words of the youngster seem to carry less weight than those of his aggressor, and the help given the victim fails to reach its objectives. In numerous situations, once again, the victim sees himself punished (in being taken out of his natural environment, for example). The victim finds himself alone to deal with the aftermath of the abuse, however painful to him or obvious to others this may be. Today, as it was yesterday, such a situation is patently unacceptable.

Health professionals, social service workers, and therapists seem on the whole ill prepared to respond to requests for help from male victims of sexual abuse. Should we be surprised at this? For some years now, the conditions surrounding women in our society have received increasing attention, and rightly so. Violence committed against women is no longer met with silence. But there has been minimal examination of the conditions for men in our society, as if men have no problems with intimacy or relationships, as if the relationships between men are not frought with violence, as if a man's situation is never problematic. To this we must add that the helping professionals and health professionals receive frequently inadequate training in matters of human sexuality. This field is often perceived as taboo or as the exclusive preserve of accredited sexologists who, it must be said, do not always have in-depth training on subjects such as sexual aggression between males. The consequence of such lacunae is a tragic failure to appreciate the repercussions of the sexual abuse of boys and an uneasiness in facing up to the reality.

Lack of knowledge is also apparent in the context of intervention with the family and relatives of the young boy to ensure his protection against the abuser, with whom in most cases contact must necessarily be severed at first. It must also be ensured that the boy is not stigmatized because of what has happened. As in cases of father-daughter incest, it may transpire in cases of father-son incest that the mother of the child feels deceived by or jealous of her son; it may also happen that a mother may be tempted to believe the denials of her spouse and to blame or punish her child. In view of the shock she is experiencing, she should be actively supported and should be encouraged to improve the mother/son relationship if at all possible. On the other hand, the boy may bear a grudge against his mother for not having believed him or protected him. These broken bridges must be rebuilt as soon as possible.

It is essential that the child who discloses himself as a victim of sexual abuse be listened to and believed by close family and social service workers. In refusing to heed the experience of sexually abused boys, one is quite likely worsening their already profound distress and, consequently, multiplying the after-effects of the abuse. The victim also needs to have his questions answered without delay. In his mind, particularly if the abuse situation is long term or the victim's first sexual experiences – he is confusing abuse and (homo)sexuality, love and genital play, affection and hatred, pain and pleasure, dependence and mistrust, etc. It is of the utmost importance that the sexually abused boy should learn how to distinguish between these phenomena. Youngsters who are experiencing homosexual or bisexual attractions have a particular need to be reassured and freed from feelings of guilt: homosexuality and bisexuality are no more synonymous with abuse than is heterosexuality. Similar sensitization is sometimes necessary on the part of their parents.

When a child is victim of intrafamilial abuse, it is very important to check that there are no other children in the same situation. Here again, the testimonies of our respondents are very eloquent: it was not unusual that brothers or sisters were going through the same nightmare, without speaking up, usually with the same abuser. And this without taking into account that some of the young victims had very soon begun to reproduce their own experiences with younger brothers or sisters. Some families have over time integrated a veritable culture of sexual abuse. It would be unreasonable to think that such a culture could instantly be brought to an end.

The minute a child reveals that he has been sexually abused, he and his family should have ready and free access to a range of pertinent therapeutic interventions. The belief that a cessation of sexual abuse ends the problems generated by it is false. It does seem, however, that the sooner a youngster and his close family are listened to and receive appropriate help, the fewer will be the after-effects.

It sometimes happens, and we have seen it, that an abused child has been subjected to abuse time and time again by different individuals. This is all the more disconcerting for the child, who begins to ask himself whether it is not, after all, normal. Because of this, psychologists and psychoanalysts have taken the position that some boys are not only more vulnerable but that they also participate, up to a certain point, in their abuse, going so far as to "seduce" the adults. This interpretation disregards the fact that the after-effects of a first abuse often explain the occurrence of further abuses. Worse still, it places on the shoulders of children a responsibility that should be borne by their aggressors. If a child becomes still more vulnerable after a first sexual abuse, it is because he has understood how it works. It is hard to see why he should be blamed for it and thenceforth be accused of debauching adults.

On the notion of purportedly voluntary seduction, authors Pauzé and Mercier have noted that to be subjected to sexual abuse by an adult is not without consequences for the relationships the child will subsequently have with other adults. Some children may sometimes engage in ways of relating based on seduction. This may be explained by the fact that these children grow up learning that sexuality constitutes their principal way of attracting others or exercising power over them, adults in particular. These children learn that to be fully accepted by the people who take care of them (be it father, friend, professor) they should engage in sexual behaviour. They come to look upon the sexual services they offer to adults as a condition of their social or familial integration.[3]

In short, the child we call "seductive" has integrated the dynamics of the abuse to such an extent that he more or less consciously tries to reproduce it, if only because he believes there is hardly any other way of relating open to him after what he has learned. This logic, then, relates to survival tactic scenarios or to adaptive strategies rather than to supposed perversions. By their own accounts, the boys and men we met who had repeatedly been victims of abuse have presented such a profile at one time or another in their lives. They know few other ways of attracting attention or gaining affection than by showing how physically charming they are. Being more or less willing to allow an adult to make use of their body had become a habit for some of them, a routine, a way of life, even if they are the first to deplore it.

It is impossible to overstate the importance of confronting the aggressor. He must be held accountable for his actions and must be confronted as soon as is reasonable. Most of the perpetrators accused by the respondents in this study have never had to answer for their acts and have consequently not been censured. Only five respondents out of thirty related that their aggressor had been reprimanded and indicted. And again, those who were found guilty were given a relatively light sentence, considering

the charges they faced. Institutions give a double message when
it comes to sexual abuse. On the legislative level they maintain
that it is a serious crime, whereas on the practical level very few
aggressors are convicted. If they are, the penalties imposed are
nominal. Only recently, a Quebec judge failed to recommend
therapy to a recidivist abuser on the grounds that he showed little
intention of amending his ways. All the more reason, Your
Honour! Perpetrators who know they will abuse again are surely
those who need the closest surveillance most. And motivation to
change can also be a therapeutic goal.

HELPING VICTIMS IN THE MEDIUM TERM AND IN THE LONG TERM

According to a number of respondents in this study, psychologists, social workers, educators, and police frequently act as
though the mere denunciation of sexual abuse brings an end to
its consequences and its aftermath. This is not so. The distress
experienced by the victim is often at its highest at the time of
denunciation. Will they believe him? What will happen to him?
How will his abuser and the people around him react? When it
involves intrafamilial abuse, the boy is anguished in the extreme
by the thought he may be responsible for the break-up of his
family or that he will be rejected and spurned by them.

As the life stories gathered here illustrate, the traumatisms and
repercussions of sexual abuse will continue to unfold long after
the abuse has ended. The abused boy remains beset by unsettling
confusion, asking questions to which he can find no answers,
harbouring a wounded identity, and relying on coping strategies
that are often ineffective. Finding solutions to these problems will
take time. Sometimes it takes as much time to assuage such hurts
as it took to develop them. Therefore, when abuse has just been
made disclosed, intervention with the ex-victim must be envisaged as a long and continuing process rather than a short-term
intervention.

Among my respondents, even when there has been some improve-
ment in their situation, many men have internalized and still main-
tained intact their distorted perceptions, their confused emotions,
and defensive strategies that may no longer be required or indicated.
Thus, some will still be closed in on themselves, hyperdistrustful,

and reclusive. Others will have learned to reverse roles in order to prove to themselves that the power, from now on, is theirs. Still others seem to take rely on the excuse of being the eternal victim, as if they cannot let go the idea that this is their fate, or as if they have been numbed by a multiplicity of painful experiences. Many are ex-victims with compulsive behaviours or long-term dependency on relationships (mostly sexual) or on substances such as drugs, alcohol, or medication. Such escape mechanisms are unfortunately among those that intrude when, deserted, the young man must protect his inner self and his social self. In the absence of a trustworthy reference, the most inappropriate social solutions seem to the ex-victim to be the logical ones.

What is evident is that some form of guidance is the most desirable form of intervention for ex-victims of sexual abuse. It allows the victim to develop self-confidence and trust in others at his own pace and to draw up plans for his life other than those magical solutions he has looked to in the past. Only through living can a life be repaired.

It is undoubtedly surprising to learn how many men who require help with personal or relationship problems have, since childhood, been dragging with them the after-effects of sexual abuse. Their difficulty, their inability to sort out present problems, often derives from their reticence to disclose their ordeal. Sometimes they have quite simply erased it from memory. To ignore or to underestimate the fall-out from sexual abuse can negate any intervention with an ex-victim. Too often the problems for which boys or adult males consult are the consequences of shameful or undisclosed traumas. It is up to helpers to carry out the necessary work of clearing the terrain: how did this boy become addicted to drugs? How did he come to detest adults, be homophobic, try to commit suicide, or mutilate himself? Behind the symptoms there is a suffering, often silent, that must be uncovered if it is to be alleviated in any lasting way.

I have often asked myself whether an ineffective coping strategy or modus vivendi could be modified if the ex-victim were made aware of its shortcomings. The material available to me does not provide answers to this question. Most current psychotherapies rest on the premise that better self-knowledge is indispensible to any attempt at self-transformation. Jean-Paul Sartre said that man was characterized above all by his ability to rise above a given situation; by what he manages to do with what others have done to him.[4]

In so far as our perception determines our attitudes, does not a different understanding of reality modify it? That said, a rational comprehension of what happens in the wake of sexual abuse is not in itself sufficient. Perceptions are one thing, emotions something quite different. Not only do the perceptions need to be changed, the emotions attached to the perceptions also need changing. Telling yourself that you are not responsible for the abuse you have endured is one thing; really to believe it is another. Nor does it follow, from knowing that love can be pleasant, that you will not be afraid when someone says he loves you. In identifying the emotions and the feelings experienced in a context of aggression, abuse survivors may come to grasp the cognitive associations that have been created. Only then will they be able to judge the significance and lasting imprint of such cognitive associations on their present conduct. Only then, in considering their significance, will they be able to decide whether or not they now wish to try and transform them.

Giving up behaviours or survival strategies that have seemed helpful in the past requires a context in which one feels safe and protected. It is impossible to proceed to a healthy questioning of one's reactions in a context that perpetuates the abuse or is reminiscent of it. In this connection I am reminded of the story of a young man I accompanied in therapy many years ago. This young man was unable to liberate himself from intrusive thoughts from the past, when he was being abused by the uncle who was "taking care" of him (his father and mother were dead). Gnawed at by guilt, haunted by paranoid delusions, he became dysfunctional, truly incapacitated. All the therapists he had consulted had withdrawn from the case. A psychiatrist was palliating his suffering with medication that rendered him even less functional. When I learned that this man was still living with his uncle's family, in the same house; that he slept in the room, even in the bed, where the aggressions had taken place, I understood that, even if his aggressor was dead, living in the same setting in which he had been abused was paralyzing him. Once out of that environment, he was able to progress surprisingly well, seeing his traumatic symptoms – nightmares, anxieties, paranoia – diminish one after another as he began trying to take charge of his own future.

I have deliberately described this man's case because it shows the importance of physically and psychologically protecting victims of sexual abuse, even long after the aggressions have ceased. Respondents who said that they had not been believed or protected by their families when they disclosed the abuse have affirmed that only a complete break with the family, however painful, had allowed them to "come out of it." Problems of negative self-esteem and negative self-image that overwhelm male victims of sexual abuse demand that they acquire a sense of having control over their own lives. This does not mean that all ties to the past should be broken. It means that links that have become chains can be broken. As one incest victim told us: "It is better to cut ties with family members rather than accept that family members do you harm every time you see them."

In helping sexual abuse survivors bring their coping strategies to light, we can encourage them to evaluate their efficacy and, if appropriate, to transform them as they go through their daily experiences. It is of prime importance for these men to develop rewarding personal relationships outside of a context reminiscent of the abuse and to avoid, above all, relationships that perpetuate in any way a submissive, dependent, or vengeful way of relating. Each man should evaluate the extent to which the survival strategies he earlier adopted really allow him to make progress today, without hurting either himself or others. Do they still meet his needs? Are there other ways to exorcise the traumas? If yes, what are the advantages? What are the risks? It is important, above all, to encourage the individual to channel his anger away from himself or others. Outlets through which human emotions may be discharged, such as artistic creativity, devotion to a cause, the practice of sports, etc., are plentiful. Any initiative that allows the ex-victim to experience personal success is beneficial, giving him openings both to the present and to the future. Thus, certain respondents have told us how encouraging it was for them to discover skills or talents they never suspected they had. Poetry, painting, music, sports, all represented for some a new and widening perspective, new horizons full of hope. The past certainly conditions, but it need not imprison. The individual always retains some freedom to chose and an ability to change.

As we have seen, undergoing sexual abuse usually carries with it a fundamental reconsideration of how the young boy sees the

world and his own masculinity. Reflecting on what it means to be
a man cannot be avoided – in particular, tackling questions about
the origin and perception of sexual abuse, relationships between
men and between the generations, gender identity, sexual orientation, and homophobia. These are all problems of essential con-
cern to ex-victims of sexual abuse. Now, if recent years have seen
the development of numerous self-help groups for men, the topic
of sexual abuse is often still taboo. It is only with diffidence that
self-help groups for adolescents or young male victims of sexual
abuse are appearing. These groups obviously cannot replace an
individual therapeutic approach when it is needed, but meeting
other men who have been abused allows each ex-victim, when he
feels ready, to discuss his own experiences and questions without
fear of being judged or marginalized. It also allows him to benefit
from others' responses and solutions. Respondents who have
participated in such groups have all spoken of profiting greatly
from the experience, if only because they felt themselves at last
fully understood by other men: precious fellow feelings.

These days, when AIDS is rampant, the ability to negotiate one's
love relationships or one's sexual relationships, while simultaneously taking into account one's needs and one's boundaries,
remains a challenge for those boys who have on the whole learned
to submit themselves to the desires of others. The results of recent
research[5] in Quebec demand some reflection. In comparing boys
who (in the initial sample) had been victims of sexual abuse
(twenty-six) to those who had never been abused (324), a team of
researchers discovered that:

– abused boys are four times more at risk of using injectable
  drugs;
– they have more sexual relations with penetration (anal or vag-
  inal) without protection against sexually transmitted disease
  (STDs) or AIDS (and practise sodomy three times more frequently than the others);
– their frequency of contracting STDs is doubled;
– they are more likely to prostitute themselves.

This disturbing picture agrees only too closely with the results of
the present study and suggests that young men who have been
victims of sexual abuse possibly constitute one of the subgroups

most at risk as far as contracting or transmitting HIV and AIDS is concerned. My own recent research on the link between risk behaviours and sexual abuse in childhood was also conclusive: male ex-victims of abuse are sometimes too passive, too confused, or too revolted to think in terms of protecting their health.[6] This subject requires more study.

A word is necessary on the Crime Victims Compensation Act, which should normally apply in cases of sexual abuse, since some respondents (in those cases where the aggressor was denounced) have complained with bitterness about the time limits imposed upon making the claim. The majority of boys I interviewed were abused at a young age and in general several years passed before the criminal act of which they were victims was denounced. Since time limits are imposed, there was no possibility of compensation. Is it not then justified, in cases of sexual abuse of minors, that the indemnification of victims of such criminal acts not be subject to any temporal limit? On the one hand, disclosure of sexual abuse is too infrequent among boys and it is often not until much later that the disclosure is made. On the other hand, victims continue to experience the aftermath of such abuse in the very long term. In the still recent past, workers taking care of these victims hardly thought about asking, in the name of the abused child, for any indemnification whatever. Certainly, material compensation cannot soften interior pain. It can, however, allow the seeking out of better services to help the victim face up to what he is going through. It is essential that the damages caused by sexual abuse be fully recognized. Too many abused boys feel that nothing has been done for them and never will be. Paradoxically, if they are to be allowed to turn the page, it must first be recognized that they have been victims.

WHEN THE EX-VICTIM IS YOUR PARTNER, YOUR BROTHER, A SON, A FRIEND OR YOURSELF

Many of us are close to someone who has been abused or live with someone who has been abused. Some of us are only too aware of it; others only suspect it but have never been able to bring up the subject; others do not know it yet. Adapting to the aftermath of abuse it not easy. Neither is it easy to live with an

ex-victim, especially if his past is still a secret that comes between
you. In this last situation you may have asked yourself in vain
for years: Where does all this inexplicable anguish come from?
Why this ambivalence in his relationships with others? If you are
a family member or a friend of a sexual abuse survivor, you are
worried to see this man at times isolating himself and at other
times behaving compulsively or aggressively towards others. If
you are in a couple relationship with one of these men, you find
yourself confronting the after-effects of abuse in your intimate
relationship with him. Lastly, if you yourself have been sexually
abused during childhood or adolescence, you are trying to rid
yourself of phantoms from the past that can reappear at any time.
How can you overcome this, put it behind you?

For weeks at a time, for months, even years, the boy victim of
sexual abuse watched himself denying his ability to say no. At an
age when he should have learned to affirm his own needs and
boundaries, he learned to keep silent. It is strongly possible that
past learning is today part of who he is, whatever the extent or
the nature of such inhibition. For example, he is so afraid of being
rejected that he will himself provoke rejection. He is insatiable
when it comes to needing affection, but at the same time, he fears
being loved. Ambiguities and uncertainties frequently torment
men who have been victims of sexual abuse. At this point their
emotional and cognitive references have been turned topsy-turvy
so that all human relations may seem threatening or dangerous.
An almost chronic distrust engulfs them: Why do we love them?
In their love relationships they are twice as wary: Why do we
desire them? Does someone want to take advantage of them
again? If they think they are losing control over just one small
portion of what is under their control, the fears and reflexes they
had as a small boy will resurface. Relationships that would seem
anodyne to most people are heavy with symbolism and anxiety
for these men. To be loved, to be touched, to be stroked, for
example, can reawaken unbearable memories.

We should remember that an abused boy has often been
betrayed by one of his close family members, so it is difficult for
him to learn to trust others again. Receiving the trust of such a
boy must be more than merited; it will be put to the test. Only
with patience and the passage of time will this test be passed
successfully. Getting close to him can be compared metaphorically

to getting close to a living burn victim. He is someone who is extremely sensitive, thin skinned, and easily hurt. No matter what you do, you will risk hurting him, or being hurt yourself by this person who, at the slightest alarm, is ready to fight to protect himself as if his life depended upon it. For this reason, you may be greatly tempted to overprotect him. This would be a mistake. Protecting him does not mean avoiding confrontation when it is necessary. A growing sense of autonomy, greater self-esteem, and a capacity to healthily affirm his needs and boundaries: these attitudes cannot be encouraged or acquired without decisive experiences and a few confrontations.

Is it possible for men who have been abused to overcome the aftermath of their experience? Certainly. As the testimony of some of the respondents indicates, among the older ones, it is possible. The traces left by new life experiences, both happy and unhappy, are continually superimposed on the memory, remodelling one's view of the world. The inscription of new memories will not wipe out the old ones, though it may sometimes give them different meanings and may even relegate them to a more distant back-drop. In the human brain each new piece of information is added to the previous and may thus contribute to a redefinition of the whole. Of course, as a person grows older it takes outstanding events or repeated experiences to bend perceptions or behaviours that are already deeply rooted. But the possibility is there for everyone. Traumas from the past will shrink such possibility but do not constitute a barrier to it. They will continue to condition the ex-victim's perceptions, reactions, and expectations. But people are not robots. Among all the possibilities, however limited they are, there are choices to be made.

We may be asking men wounded by sexual abuse to show a force of character and a courage of which few of us are capable. False solutions are numerous, as are the traps that lie in wait for these men, and it is quite difficult to escape from a trap if you are unaware of its existence. It would be unreasonable to think that one could wipe out the aftermath of sexual abuse simply by willing it. The reprogramming of relationship, love, or sexual scripts that have been under construction since childhood and adolescence would be a long and arduous undertaking, if indeed we concede it possible. Since sexual abuse may act as a learning experience in virility and sexuality for certain boys, it is likely to leave some impressions that will be hard to erase. Not only do those impressions become part of the person, they also help to shape his ways of perceiving and behaving.

If you are the partner or the friend of a man who was sexually abused in childhood, it could be that the reasons, conscious or not, for which you find yourself in the relationship also have a bearing on your own trauma. Acquaintances and affinities are rarely the fruit of hazard. Without necessarily sharing the same wounds – although this may also be a possibility – you have sensed in him something that reverberates in you. Perhaps you also have a tendency to see yourself as a victim, perhaps you want to be a rescuer, perhaps you admire his temerity, etc. Whatever it may be, your complementary aspects describe his needs as well as your own. This reminds me of a young girl who had done the impossible in order that her lover, an ex-victim of abuse, should undertake therapy in order to deal with his anxieties. The snag was that she did not recognize in him, afterwards, the person she had chosen to be her partner: he had changed "too much." The couple broke up without her knowing really why. She had wanted to rescue him, but once he had undertaken to rescue himself, she had found herself useless, set aside.

Sharing the life of a sexual abuse victim in some way involves accepting that you will be cross-examined, because his constant doubts and questioning will sooner or later affect those who are close to him. Not to mention, of course, that all introspective work requires a certain isolation. The abused boy has been so perturbed that, even years later, he does not know exactly who he is, what he wants, what he feels, what he loves, or what he hates. Learning to listen to himself and to identify his own needs is a first step towards finding himself. It is only later that he will learn to communicate his expectations and to negotiate around them in his personal relationships, provided those involved can tolerate the reciprocity.

Thus, the efforts made by an ex-victim to redefine himself may just as well prove to be an opportunity to get closer to or reconcile with others as much as they may cause a distancing or breaking up. Giving up irrational anxieties, fears, or destructive behaviours may permit the ex-victim to be more available to his closest family and even to see in them something other than he had earlier perceived. Learning to share emotions and feelings without fear can allow a man who was formerly distant, secretive, or inward looking to communicate better. Sometimes, it will also entail settling certain accounts from the past and bringing about drastic changes, not without embarrassment to his family. All change implies some form of crisis. One never knows what may come out of it.

Whether male or female, being a sexual abuse victim has nothing to do with destiny or being under a curse. It is a chance happening during the course of someone's life, tragic certainly, but an accident all the same. As with all accidents, a certain readaptation is called for. Psychological or relational handicaps are less visible than physical handicaps but they are often more disabling, especially when nothing is done to counterbalance them. This book provides no miracle solution because there is none. It describes a reality, sketches profiles, explains the dynamics. This understanding will not serve as a tool to bring about change except to the extent that it may be fleshed out, given shape, embodied. To be an ex-victim or to share the life of an ex-victim is somewhat like having to relearn the business of life and how to live it. In short, it is to dare to educate ourselves out of our own pain and the pain of others.

Epilogue

I wrote this book in order to better understand a little-known phenomenon and to share my discoveries about it. Some partial answers emerge from this study, but many questions remain. For example: To what extent does recall exist in the body and memory? Exactly what roles are played by the cognitive impressions left behind by a sexual aggression? If the past cannnot be erased, how may its after-effects be dealt with? Are there therapies or processes that would enable the sexually abused boy to turn the page once and for all? We are only just now beginning to find fragments of the answers.

It is usual to end a study of this sort by reminding the reader of its limitations. I perceive two. The first relates to my research method, which is the gathering of life stories. Is it possible that, in recounting his life, a victim might, while trying to make some kind of sense out of it, begin to create a script from it? It is impossible to know. Certainly, our recollection of the past is made up of so many choices, avoidances, short-cuts, and imaginings that the story we each make of our life is necessarily subjective and adapted, more or less consciously, to the individual's subsequent evolution. No one escapes this process: in recalling our past, we select and we reinterpret. But this element of subjectivity does not consist of negative aspects alone. On the contrary, in recounting the past, we spontaneously accord priority to those events we consider the most telling, the most essential. The texture of the narrative, the words expressing it, the emotion within it, all these give back to the person who is telling the story what he was and what he has become. The past is recreated each time it is retold.

How could it be otherwise? Rather than ask what objectivity is lost in the telling, let us ask what the story brings us in the way of pertinent and high quality information.

A second reservation concerns the sample of volunteers who collaborated in the research, and how representative they are. As I have already pointed out, there is presently no means of choosing a sample that is representative of all the boys and men who have been victims of sexual abuse. The phenomenon remains too clandestine, too unrecognized, and probably too underestimated for anyone to be able to determine what such a sample would look like. As in the majority of studies dealing with questions of sexuality and intimacy, it has been necessary to fall back on voluntary participation. This procedure is often criticized for the fact that voluntary participants might have a tendency to be "exhibitionist," that is, to insist on telling their story to the world and then possibly to exaggerate. All I can say is that I have never received such an impression from the people I have interviewed. On the contrary, in many cases I was one of the very first in whom they confided, their initial restraint diminishing as a climate of trust was born. I came across no example of exaggeration or lies. What's more, the spontaneity with which these voluntary respondents replied to my questions in spite of the bad memories and the sadness those questions evoked leads me to believe in their complete good faith.

Could the results of this study be generalized to a broader population? For the reasons I have just laid out, we must consider my research as exploratory. I believe, however, that it allows a considerable step to be taken toward gaining a better understanding of the behavioural and relationship dynamics of boys who have been victims of sexual abuse.

I had thought it would be difficult to find volunteers to participate in the research, but I was amazed to learn at the end of nearly every one of the interviews I carried out that the respondents described themselves as satisfied, even happy with our conversation. I have given some serious thought to this reaction: after all, we had just spent an hour and a half talking about some of the most unhappy events in their lives. I soon understood that in retracing their history with them I was indirectly helping them reshape the puzzle that is their life, to make connections between what they had lived and what they had become. If it is true that we are our experiences, then understanding our history and its ongoing implications is vital for those who wish to better direct the future. Most of the men I interviewed had intuitively understood this.

One by one, their stories move or shock us. If they illustrate the dramas experienced in the lives of boy victims of sexual abuse, they also illustrate the great diversity of the resulting after-effects and of the ways they have been dealt with. Each life history is unique, as is each of us because of our individual strengths and weaknesses.

It might seem odd that carrying out research on such a troubling subject should ultimately prove gratifying and enriching. Such, however, is the case. One cannot emerge unchanged from such an undertaking. Although I myself was never sexually abused, I experienced a solidarity with those who carry this wound. I hope that other researchers will become interested in the fate of boy victims of sexual abuse. It is of the utmost urgency to perfect the measures to be taken against abusers and to come to the help of their victims. In order to do this we need to refine our understanding of the male experience of sexual abuse and of its multiple implications.

Sexual abuse is one of the worst torments a human being, male or female, can undergo, because it attacks the victim's physical and psychological integrity at the same time. We are only beginning to discover its meanings and repercussions, especially where boys or young men are concerned. For these survivors, who apprehensively seek to know who they really are, much remains to be done. The long journey is only just beginning.

Appendices

Profile of Respondents in Sample

Lifting the veil of silence that hides the masculine experience of sexual abuse was not without methodological difficulty. To maximize the project's chances of being successful it was essential to find men who were ready to speak with a certain openness about the sexual abuse they had undergone, to tap into diverse sources of respondents, and to find men who were willing to devote the amount of time required to answer my questions. Requests were sent out to the following: a network of group homes of youth in difficulty (eleven respondents, in fact the youngest, come from these establishments); therapy groups for men (six respondents); and community newspapers; and persons interested in this problem (thirteen respondents).

No one will deny that this sample, made up of volunteers, is in all likelihood not truly representative of all male victims of sexual abuse. It also harbours a certain bias in that more than half the respondents are or were in the past in helping relationships.

My only absolute criteria were that the respondent had to have been a victim of sexual abuse perpetrated by older adolescents or adult men during childhood or adolescence – and this from their own point of view[1] – and that the respondent had now to be between sixteen and forty-four years of age.[2]

Confidentiality and anonymity were guaranteed. The tapes and transcriptions were kept under lock and key, identified by means of a pseudonym chosen by the respondent. The length of each interview was adapted to the availability and rhythm of each respondent, an average of about one hour and a half.

Total number of respondents: 30
Average age at time of interview: 24 years, 6 months

Average age at time of first abuse: 8 years, 4 months
Place of residence at time abuse   Half the respondents lived in an
   was reported: urban milieu and half in a
                                 semi-urban or rural milieu.

Types of abuse reported:
Intergenerational and intrafamilial abuse: 15
Father-son incest:
   (Paul, Charles, Jimmy, Francis, Andrew, Justin, Robert, Harold)   8
Pseudo-incest (father substitute):
   (Bruno, Maxim, Patrick, Eric)   4
Abuse committed by another adult male in the family:
   (Justin [uncle], Jean-Philipe [uncle], Frederick [grandfather])   3

Intergenerational and extrafamilial abuse: 9
Abuse committed by a third party adult:
   Dennis (skating-rink superintendent)
   Matthew (father of best friend)
   Pascal (friend of family)
   Marcel (elderly neighbour)
   Vladimir (stranger, in schoolyard)
   James (adult who took him in whenever he ran away)
   John-Paul (handicapped friend of father)
   Eric (friends of substitute father, then social service educators)
   Oliver (his mother's boyfriend)

Intragenerational and intrafamilial abuse: 7
Incest between brothers:
   (Paul, Peter, Joseph, Jean-Sylvain, Justin)   5
Abuse by a cousin or young uncle:
   (Jean-Marc, Oliver)   2

Intragenerational and extrafamilial abuse: 4
Abuse committed by older but not adult third party:
   Martin (friends when he was a runaway)
   Steve (adolescent neighbours)
   Serge (adolescent friend)
   Antoine (neighbour aged sixteen)

Research Method

The research method employed in this qualitative study is inspired by the sociological approach of the Chicago School,[1] by anthroposociology of the experience,[2] and, to a certain extent, by clinical sociology.[3] The goal of the research was to grasp the felt experience of the men I interviewed, using an analysis of these cases. A symbolic-interactionist[4] conceptual framework was used in the analysis. As its name implies, a symbolic-interactionist paradigm postulates that social life is made up of interactions to which meanings are attached, this being how sense is made of human conduct and of the ensuing reactions to it. A certain strategic analysis[5] has grafted itself to this perspective, focusing the attention of the researcher on the cost-benefit relationships inherent in every human decision and in each human reaction, particularly in power relationships.

I usually met alone with the respondents in an office reserved for the purpose. Sometimes the meeting took place at the respondent's home. The majority of conversations were taped and transcribed verbatim. In keeping with the principles of grounded theory and inductive analysis,[6] the data were processed as soon as they were obtained so that new material could be compared with what had been previously gathered, and vice versa. Analysis of the material allowed me to separate out key events, recurring patterns of experience, and outlines of behaviours (which often provide the subtitles in this work). The conclusions I drew in the process were compared with the results of other studies (most of which are quantitative) and discussed with specialists in the field as well as with male victims of childhood sexual abuse other than the respondents. The text of each story has been structured chronologically in order to facilitate its comprehension and to respect the most elementary rules of written language (though various current colloquialisms have been left as is). The study took place in the middle of the 1990s.

Notes

CHAPTER ONE

1 E. Badinter, XY, de l'identité masculine (Paris: Odile Jacob, 1992) 57.
2 A more detailed respondent profile is given at Appendix 1.
3 In order to specify the similarities and differences in the after-effects of heterosexual and homosexual abuse, it would be necessary to carry out a comparative study that would include male victims of childhood sexual abuse perpetrated by women.
4 M.P. Mendel, The Male Survivor (Thousand Oaks: Sage, 1995); J. Gonsiorek et al., Male Sexual Abuse (Thousand Oaks: Sage, 1994).
5 D. Welzer-Lang, Le viol au masculin (Paris: L'Harmattan, 1988), 23.
6 B. Watkins and A. Bentovim, "The Sexual Abuse of Male Children and Adolescents: A Review of Current Reserach," Journal of Child Psychology and Psychiatry 23, 1:197.
7 T. Sandfort et al., Male Intergenerational Intimacy (New York: Harrington Press, 1991).
8 Sue Clegg, "Studying Child Sexual Abuse: Morality or Science?" Radical Philosophy no. 66 (Spring 1994).

CHAPTER TWO

1 Government of Canada, "Sexual Offences against Children: Report of the Committee on Sexual Offences against Children and Youth (Ottawa: Canadian Government Publications Centre, Supply and Services Canada, 1984), 1:180.
2 See reviews of the literature carried out by F.G. Bolton and others in Males at Risk (Newbury Park: Sage, 1989), 41; by W. Breer in Diagnosis and Treatment of the Young Male Victim of Sexual Abuse

(Springfield, IL: Charles C. Thomas, 1992), 14, 190; and by
   C. Violato and M. Genius, "Problems of Research in Male Sexual
   Abuse: A Review," *Journal of Child Sexual Abuse* 2 (1993).
 3 D. Finkelhor et al., "Sexual Abuse in a National Survey of Adult
   Men and Women," in *Child Abuse and Neglect* 14, no. 1 (1990):19–28.
 4 A.J.C. King, R.P. Beazley, et al., *Canada Youth and AIDS Studies*
   (Kingston: Queen's University, 1988).
 5 See review of the literature by B. Watkins and A. Bentovim, "Male
   Children and Adolescents as Victims: A Review of Current Knowledge," in *Male Victims of Sexual Assault*, edited by G.G. Mezey
   (Oxford: Oxford University Press, 1992).
 6 J. Lever, "Sexual Revelations," *The Advocate*, nos. 661–2 (23 August
   1994).
 7 According to D.S. Everstine and L. Everstine, *Sexual Trauma in
   Children and Adolescents* (New York: Brunner/Mazel, 1989), 131.
   The Report of the Committee on Sexual Offences against Children
   and Youth (see note 1, above) suggests the figure of 28.2 percent
   of the number of cases.
 8 J.M. Masson, *Le réel escamoté* (Paris: Aubier, 1984).
 9 B. Cyrulnik, *Sous le signe du lien* (Paris: Hachette, 1989), 241–2.
 10 H. Parker and S. Parker, "Father Daughter Sexual Abuse: An
   Emerging Perspective," *American Journal of Orthopsychiatry* 54,
   no. 14 (1986):531–49.
 11 G.M. Sarotte, *Like a Brother, Like a Lover: Male Homosexuality in the
   American Novel and Theatre from Herman Melville to James Baldwin*,
   translated from the French by Richard Miller (Garden City, NY:
   Anchor Press/Doubleday, 1978).

CHAPTER THREE

 1 Cited in M. Gabel, *Les enfants victimes d'abus sexuels* (Paris: PUF,
   1992), 72–4.
 2 C. Hubberstey, *A Phenomenological Study of Men Who Have Experienced Sexual Abuse in Childhood or Adolescence*, master's thesis,
   University of Victoria, British Columbia, 1988.

CHAPTER FOUR

 1 D. Welzer-Lang, "L'homophobie: la face cachée du masculin," in
   D. Welzer-Lang, P. Dutey and M. Dorais, *La peur de l'autre en soi*,
   (Montreal: VLB, 1994), 23–30.

2 M. Godelier, *La production des Grands Hommes* (Paris: Fayard, 1982), 91–2.
3 R.J. Stoller, *Presentations of Gender* (New Haven: Yale University Press, 1985). The text quoted is based on the research of G. Herdt.
4 See also B. Sergent, *L'homosexualité initiatique dans l'Europe ancienne* (Paris: Payot, 1986).
5 P. Veyne, "L'homosexualité à Rome," in *Amour et sexualité en Occident*, edited by G. Duby (Paris: Seuil, 1991).
6 D. Welzer-Lang et al., *La peur de l'autre en soi* (Montreal: VLB, 1994).
7 J. Brière and M. Runtz, "University Males' Interest in Children," *Child Abuse and Neglect* 13 (1989):65–75.
8 M. Dorais, *Les lendemains de la révolution sexuelle* (Montreal: VLB, 1990). See in particular the chapter entitled "Une impérieuse pulsion."
9 D.S. Everstine and L. Everstine, *Sexual Trauma in Children and Adolescents* (New York: Brunner/Mazel, 1989), 139.
10 E. Brongersma, *Loving Boys*, 2 vols. (Elmhurst: New York, Global Academic Publishers, 1986, 1990); T. O'Carroll, *Paedophilia – The Radical Case* (Boston: Alyson, 1982); T. Sandfort, *The Sexual Aspect of Paedophile Relations* (Amsterdam: Pan/Spartacus, 1982); and T. Sandfort et al., *Male Intergenerational Intimacy* (New York: Harrington Press, 1991).
11 Eva Cantarella, *Bisexuality in the Ancient World* (New Haven, CT: Yale University Press, 1994).
12 Suetonius, *The Twelve Caesars* (New York: Penguin Classics, 1991), 3:44.
13 D.Welzer-Lang et al., *La peur de l'autre en soi* (Montreal: VLB, 1994), 29–30.
14 S. Brownmiller, *Against Our Will: Men, Women and Rape* (New York: Simon and Schuster, 1975).
15 Rollo May, *Love and Will* (New York: W.W. Norton, 1969).

CHAPTER FIVE

1 The title derives from Stefan Zweig's novel *La confusion des sentiments* (Paris, Gallimard, 1983).
2 M. Mendel, *The Male Survivor* (Thousand Oaks: Sage, 1995); J. Brière and M. Runtz, "Suicidal Thoughts and Behaviours in Former Sexual Abuse Victims," in *Canadian Journal of Behavioural Science*, no. 18 (1986):413–23.

3 N. Groth, *Men Who Rape* (New York: Plenum Press, 1979), 123.
4 Ibid., 139.
5 M. Hunter, *Abused Boys* (New York: Fawcett Colombine, 1990), 86.
6 G.C. Mezey and M.B. King, *Male Victims of Sexual Assault* (Oxford: Oxford University Press, 1992), 53.
7 M. Hunter, *Abused Boys*, 85.
8 The passage that R. Pauzé and J. Mercier devote to this phenomenon and its repercussions in their work *Les aggressions sexuelles à l'égard des enfants* (Montreal: Saint-Martin, 1994), 161–6, is enlightening. False complaints often differ most significantly from others in the sense that the testimonies of the children are devoid of emotion, the children are free from after-effects, and, in the cases where incest is alleged, the parents are already in a dispute over custody.

CHAPTER SIX

1 A. Mucchielli, *L'identité* (Paris: PUF, 1992).
2 H.R. Fuchs Ebaugh, *Becoming an Ex* (Chicago: University of Chicago Press, 1988).
3 H.M. Lips and N.L. Colwill, *The Psychology of Sex Differences* (Englewood Cliffs, NJ: Prentice Hall, 1978); J. Money, *Gendermaps* (New York: Continuum, 1995); R. Stoller, *Presentations of Gender* (New Haven: Yale University Press, 1985), and R. Stoller, *Observing the Erotic Imagination* (New Haven: Yale University Press, 1985).
4 C. Chiland, "L'identité sexuée en Occident" in *Nouvelle Revue d'Ethno-psychiatrie – Marques sexuelles*, no. 18, (Paris: La Pensée sauvage, 1991).
5 E. Erikson, *Childhood and Society* (Middlesex: Penguin Books, 1965).
6 N. Groth, *Men Who Rape* (New York: Plenum Press, 1979) 140.
7 Florence Rush, *The Best Kept Secret: Sexual Abuse of Children* (Englewood Cliffs, NJ: Prentice Hall, 1980), 170.
8 D. Welzer-Lang, *Le viol au masculin* (Paris: L'Harmattan, 1988), 194.
9 Robert J. Stoller, *Presentations of Gender*.
10 D. Finkelhor, "Four Preconditions: a Model," in Finkelhor's *Child Sexual Abuse: New Theory and Research* (New York: Free Press, 1984).
11 R.L. Johnson and D.K. Schrier, "Sexual Victimization of Boys: Experience at an Adolescent Medicine Clinic," *Journal of Adolescent Health Care* 6 (1985):372–6.

12 D. Welzer-Lang, "L'homophobie: la face cachée du masculin," in
   D. Welzer-Lang, P. Dutey, and M. Dorais, *La peur de l'autre en soi*
   (Montreal: VLB, 1994).
13 Quoted in E. Jansen, "Daddy Dearest," *Genre* 21 (September
   1994):37.
14 Stoller, *Presentations of Gender.*
15 W.E. Prendergast, *Sexual Abuse of Children and Adolescents* (New
   York: Continuum, 1996), 296–7.
16 J. Lever, "Sexual Revelations," *The Advocate* (23 August 1994).
17 D. Welzer-Lang et al., *La peur de l'autre en soi* (Montreal: VLB, 1994).
18 For a critique of this perspective, refer to my article "La recherche
   des causes de l'homosexualité: une science fiction?" in D. Welzer-
   Lang, et al., *La peur de l'autre en soi.*
19 M.F. Myers, "Men Sexually Assaulted as Adults and Sexually
   Abused as Boys, *Archives of Sexual Behaviour* 18, no. 3 (1989).
20 J. Sebold, "Indicators of Child Sexual Abuse in Males," *Social
   Casework* 68 (February 1987):75–80.
21 C. Gentaz, "L'homophobie masculine," in D. Welzer-Lang et al.,
   La peur de l'autre en soi.

CHAPTER SEVEN

1 J. Lewis Herman, *Trauma and Recovery* (New York: Basic Books,
   1992), 51–6.
2 For a succinct summary of this approach, see "L'acteur et ses
   logiques," *Sciences humaines*, no. 9 (May-June 1995):15. Strategic
   analysis has been developed in particular by the French sociologist
   Michel Crozier. Quebec criminologist Maurice Cusson has made an
   interesting application of strategic analysis in *Délinquants, pourquoi?* (Montreal: Hurtubise HMH, 1981).
3 Government of Canada, *Sexual Offences against Children: Report of the
   Committee on Sexual Offences against Children and Youth* (Ottawa:
   Canadian Government Publications Centre, Supply and Services
   Canada, 1984), 2:978.
4 "Youth Prostitution," in *Child Pornography and Sex Rings*, edited by
   A.W. Burgess (Lexington: Lexington Books, 1984).
5 R. Stoller, *Perversion: The Erotic Form of Hatred* (New York: Pantheon
   Books, c.1975), 105.
6 W.E. Prendergast, *Sexual Abuse of Children and Adolescents* (New
   York: Continuum, 1996), 50–1.

7 Alberto Moravia, *The Conformist: A Novel*, translated by Angus
  Davidson. (New York: Farrar, Straus and Young, 1951. Reprint,
  Westport, CT: Greenwood Press, 1975).
8 S. Tisseron, *La honte* (Paris: Dunod, 1992), 76.

CHAPTER EIGHT

1 M.D. Everson and B.W. Boat, "False Allegations of Sexual Abuse by
  Children and Adolescents," in *Journal of American Academy of Child
  and Adolescent Psychiatry* 28 (1989):230–5.
2 This judge was appointed chief justice a very short time later, without doubt in recognition of her excellent professional judgment.
3 R. Pauzé and J. Mercier, *Les agressions sexuelles à l'égard des enfants*
  (Montreal: Editions Saint-Martin, 1994), 17.
4 Jean-Paul Sartre, *Critique of Dialectical Reason*, 2 vols. Vol. 1: *Theory
  of Practical Ensembles*, translated by Alan Sheridan-Smith (London:
  NLB; Atlantic Highlands, New Jersey: Humanities Press, 1976).
  Vol. 2: *The Intelligibility of History*, translated by Quinton Hoare
  (London, New York: Verso, 1991).
5 F. Pilote, J. Otis, E. Roy, and J.-Y. Frappier, "Les jeunes victimes
  d'abus sexuels par le passé seraient-ils plus vulnérables à l'infec-
  tion du VIH," ACFAS, Chicoutimi, 26 May 1995.
6 My research, funded by Health and Welfare Canada, on risk behaviour related to spread of HIV in young sexually abused men who
  have homosexual relations ("Les conduites à risque de transmission du VIH chez des jeunes hommes ayant subis des agressions
  sexuelles et ayant des rapports homosexuels") was published
  in *La Revue Sexologique/Sexological Review* 6 (Autumn 1998):2.
  An English summary is available from the author at
  Michel.Dorais@svs.ulaval.ca and an English version of the article
  will be published soon.

APPENDIX ONE

1 A similar perspective has already been used in an American study
  where the young volunteers were required, as a first characteristic,
  to have every reason to believe they had already been sexually
  abused. J.R. Conte and J.R. Schuerman, "The Effects of Sexual
  Abuse on Children," in *Lasting Effects of Child Sexual Abuse*, edited
  by G.E. Wyatt and G.J. Powell (Newbury Park: Sage, 1988).

2 I have arbitrarily taken the age of forty-four to be descriptive of a still-young adult.

APPENDIX TWO

1 A. Coulon, *L'Ecole de Chicago* (Paris: PUF, 1992); J. Peneff, *La Méthode Biographique* (Arman Colin, 1990).

2 F. Dubet, *Sociologie de l'experience* (Paris: Seuil, 1994).

3 E. Enriquez et al., *L'analyse clinique dans les sciences humaines* (Montreal: Éditions Saint-Martin, 1993); V. de Gaulejac and S. Roy, *Sociologies cliniques* (Paris: Hommes et perspectives, 1993).

4 A.Strauss, *La trame de la négociation: sociologie qualitative et interactionnisme* (Paris: L'Harmattan, 1992); H. Becker, *Outsiders* (Glencoe: Free Press, 1963); J.H. Gagnon and W. Simon, *Sexual Conduct* (Chicago: Aldine, 1973).

5 See especially M. Crozier and E. Friedberg, *L'acteur et le système* (Paris: Seuil, 1977); M. Cusson, *Délinquants, pourquoi?* (Montreal: Hurtubise HMH, 1981).

6 For more information on this topic, consult my article entitled "Diversité et créativité en recherche qualitative" in *Service Social* 42, no. 2 (1993):7–27.

Index

89, 99, 111, 141, 147,
163; characteristic(s),
62; empathetic, 91;
having sex with chil-
dren, 25; partner(s),
59; protective, 91;
respected, 47; sexual
desire(s) of, 45; sexual
demand(s) of, 46;
sexuality, 148
advances, 47, 147
Advocate, The, 17, 118
affection(s), 28, 29, 40,
43, 44, 45, 46, 47, 54,
59, 71, 82, 87, 128,
132, 146, 154, 155, 158,
167; lack of, 49, 73;
parental, 83; search
for, 70; sexualized, 45,
47, 49; showed, 71
affectionate, 102, 153
after-effect(s), 4, 5, 8, 66,
81, 96, 120, 137, 151,
154, 159, 166, 167, 169;
physical, 94; psycho-
somatic, 94
agenda: hidden, 147
aggression(s): 46, 50, 55,
61, 63, 66, 69, 70, 100,
111, 136, 138, 170
aggressor(s): 18, 20, 22,
23, 27, 28, 29, 30, 32,
42, 43, 44, 45, 47, 59,
62, 63, 64, 65, 66, 67,
68, 69, 70, 83, 84, 85,
86, 88, 89, 90, 95, 110,
111, 112, 113, 114, 117,
119, 140, 141, 142, 143,
144, 160, 161, 162, 163,
166, 167, 171
AIDS, 32, 40, 41, 172, 173
Alan, 54, 55
alcohol, 4, 79, 87, 92, 95,
99, 108, 125, 155, 156,
157
allegations: false, 164
ambiguity, 121

ambivalence, 44, 50,
121, 123
American parent
groups, 96
amnesia, 95, 151
anaesthetizing: feel-
ing(s), 87; pain, 92
Andrew: 26, 64, 69, 88,
91, 184; story, 77–80
androgynous, 113, 117
anger, 51, 56, 62, 63,
113, 144
anguish, 90, 95, 136
anxiety, 65, 89, 95, 123,
124
Antoine, 32, 88, 184
appearance(s), 150;
normal, 149, 151
apprenticeship, 61, 142
army, 69, 107; cadet(s),
107, 108, 133
arousal, 73, 78
arrests, 74, 100; of
father, 37
asexual, 51, 53
assault, 70
attachment, 43, 47, 85,
137
attention, 44, 45, 46, 47,
49, 51, 54, 59, 71, 82,
83, 102, 117, 131, 132,
167
attraction: towards
children, 52; towards
males, 77; towards
men, 50
authority, 144, 153
autonomy, 110

Badgley Commission,
16, 139
Badinter, Elizabeth, 4
Baruya(s), 60
Batman and Robin,
144–7; syndrome,
145
beating: 56, 68, 69

beauty: canon(s) of, 52,
53, 62
behaviour(s), 26, 38, 60,
75, 83, 133, 138, 139,
143, 149, 150, 152, 153;
aggressive, 162; com-
pulsive, 169; escapist,
140; exhibitionist, 94;
problem(s), 37; self-
destructive, 62
benefactor(s), 32, 71
betrayal, 29, 71, 78,
89–91, 103, 108, 147,
154, 174
bisexuality, 16, 18, 66, 166
bisexual, 42, 53, 65,
89, 101, 116, 117, 118,
120, 124, 151, 158;
as potential abuser(s),
121; orientation, 93,
146; tendencies, 144
bitterness, 70
blackmail: emotional,
44; financial, 44
body, 44, 45, 46, 52, 57,
62, 65, 68, 71, 72, 79,
83–5, 87, 89, 94, 98, 103,
111, 125, 131, 146, 147,
149, 167; awareness,
84, 110; building, 113
brain, 65, 136
breastfeeding, 60
Briere, J, and M. Runtz,
61
brother(s), 29–32, 42, 43,
50, 52, 67, 77, 83, 85,
86, 87, 97, 125, 129,
145; in-law, 157; Jean-
Sylvain's, 30, 31;
Joseph's, 30, 70; Jus-
tin's, 30, 153–8; older,
51, 67, 70; Paul's, 30,
130–5; Pierre's, 30, 70
Bruno, 18, 19, 25, 26, 46,
85, 123, 149, 151, 184;
story, 125–9
brutality, 69, 139

material, 139; psycho-
logical, 88; physical,
88
rite(s): of passage, 59;
secret, 64
ritual(s): of initiation, 64
Robert, 25, 26, 184
role(s), 38; aggressive,
79; social-sexual, 60
role model, 55, 86, 142,
145
rule(s), 61
runaway, 43, 71, 91
Rush, Florence, 114

sacrifice, 132
sadomasochism, 148
Sambia(s), 60
Sarotte, Georges Michel,
29
Sartre, Jean-Paul, 169–70
satisfaction, 87, 116, 134,
139
scare, 57, 78
school, 50, 51, 55, 78, 79,
90, 103, 127
Sebold, John, 121
secret, 3, 4, 17, 27, 46,
47, 50, 58, 59–62, 68,
75, 90, 93, 99, 105,
111, 117, 125, 140, 143,
147, 174
security, 137
seducer, 150
seduction, 90, 150, 166,
167
self, 4, 84, 93, 109, 112,
128, 141
self-assurance, 99, 150,
155
self-confidence, 169
self-defense, 54
self-destruction, 85
self-discovery, 119
self-disgust, 92
self-esteem, 92, 110, 114,
141, 157

self-image, 109
self-mutilation, 62, 68,
84, 107, 140, 150
self-punishment, 84
semen, 60
sensation(s), 49, 136;
erotic, 88
sentence, 41, 167
sentimentality, 66
Serge, 20, 32, 43, 184
sex, 35, 36, 46, 48, 49,
50, 58, 61, 62, 74, 75,
77, 78, 79, 91, 94, 98,
99, 100, 101, 103, 104,
105, 107, 112, 117, 125,
127, 132; addict(s),
129; biological, 115;
forced, 142; maniac,
74, 127, 128; slave,
139
sexologist(s), 165
sexual abuse, xi, xii, 5,
9, 16, 17, 21, 26, 33,
42–8, 59, 62, 64, 65,
66, 67, 68, 72, 78, 81,
82, 83, 89, 91, 97, 108,
109, 117, 118, 121, 136,
137, 140, 141, 151, 153,
159, 166, 168; acts, 10,
16; as continuous pro-
cess, 47; as collective
problem, 163; as form
of initiation into mas-
culinity, 61; at home,
34, 35, 49; between
males, 5, 61; child
survivors of, ix;
definition of, 6–8;
dynamic(s), 47, 48;
four phases of, 47;
of boys, ix, x, xii, 4, 5,
6, 17, 21, 42, 82, 96,
160; of children, 139;
origin of, 172; out-
come, 47; perception,
172; survivor(s), 174
sexual abuser(s), 10, 88

sexual act(s), 7, 10, 17,
27, 32, 40, 44, 46, 52,
55, 57, 60, 61, 64, 65,
68, 69, 72, 73, 74, 77,
78, 79, 87, 88, 89, 93,
97, 102, 103, 104, 105,
116, 121, 126, 131, 132,
133, 139, 142, 148, 153,
155, 157, 164, 172
sexual activity(ies), 6,
36, 53, 79, 155; forced,
59, 67
sexual agression, 9, 16,
30, 63, 64, 65, 113,
118, 139; between
males, 165
sexual arousal, 67, 136,
148
sexual behavior, 118;
involvement of
minors in, 8; normal,
63
sexual compulsivity, 140
sexual consent: age of, 8
sexual desire(s), 111
sexual dysfunction(s), 95
sexual education, 64, 66,
159; of aggressor(s),
162; lack of, 35, 162;
of victim(s), 162
sexual encounter(s), 49,
84, 98; frequency of, 49
sexual experience(s), 31,
98, 134
sexual favour(s), 47, 83,
103
sexual gratification, 63,
83
sexual initiation, 17,
64–6; forced, 61
sexual need(s), 61, 84,
111
sexual object(s), 65, 67,
84, 111, 139
sexual orientation, 6, 42,
90, 109, 112, 115–20,
158, 172